Building Blocks

A Legislator's Guide to Child Care Policy

by

Mary L. Culkin
Scott Groginsky
Steve Christian

National Conference of State Legislatures
William T. Pound, Executive Director

1560 Broadway, Suite 700
Denver, Colorado 80202

444 North Capitol Street, N.W., Suite 515
Washington, D.C. 20001

December 1997

The National Conference of State Legislatures serves the legislators and staffs of the nation's 50 states, its commonwealths, and territories. NCSL is a bipartisan organization with three objectives:

- To improve the quality and effectiveness of state legislatures,
- To foster interstate communication and cooperation,
- To ensure states a strong cohesive voice in the federal system.

The Conference operates from offices in Denver, Colorado, and Washington, D.C.

Printed on recycled paper

CONTENTS

PREFACE AND ACKNOWLEDGMENTS

Building Blocks: A Legislator's Guide to Child Care Policy is a product of the Child Care Project of the National Conference of State Legislatures. The project's primary mission is to provide state legislators with information and technical assistance about early childhood care and education issues.

We are grateful for the support of The Pew Charitable Trusts and Linda Rich, Program Officer and the A.L. Mailman Family Foundation and Luba Lynch, Executive Director, who have recognized that state lawmakers are instrumental in promoting the importance of early childhood policies.

The authors wish to thank the members of the Blue Ribbon Advisory Panel on Child Care who have worked diligently with the authors to develop this guide, including reviewing drafts. The reviewers are not responsible for the final product, but their perspectives undoubtedly improved the document both in content and structure. Members of the panel include: Representatives Sheryl Allen of Utah, Mary Brennan of Florida, John Gard of Wisconsin, Charleta B. Tavares of Ohio and Mary Jane Wallner of New Hampshire, Senator Virginia Foxx of North Carolina, Jack Hailey of the California Senate Office of Research, Richard M. Clifford of the Frank Porter Graham Center, Harriet Dichter of the Philadelphia Citizens for Children and Youth, Mark Greenberg of the Center for Law and Social Policy, Sarah Greene of the National Head Start Association, Anne Mitchell of Early Childhood Policy Research, Michele Piel of the Illinois Department of Human Services, Doug Price of First Bank of Colorado and Gail Richardson of the Child Care Action Campaign.

The authors also wish to thank those who assisted in reviewing this document. Specific thanks go to: Gina Adams and Helen Blank of the Children's Defense Fund, Ellen Galinsky of the Families and Work Institute, Andrea Genser and Gwen Morgan of the Wheelock College Center for Career Development in Early Care and Education, Linda Rich of The Pew Charitable Trusts, Steve Savner of the Center for Law and Social Policy, Larry Schweinhart of the High/Scope Educational Research Foundation, Louise Stoney of Stoney Associates, Sally Vogler of the Colorado Governor's office and Marcy Whitebook of the National Center for the Early Childhood Workforce.

Several NCSL Children and Families Program staff contributed to this publication. Laurie McConnell provided extensive research and analysis; Dana Reichert assisted with research; Jack Tweedie provided editing and guidance; and Barbara Houlik assisted with administrative support. NCSL Human Services Committee Director Sheri Steisel assisted with editing. Overall editing was provided by NCSL book editor Leann Stelzer. Cover design and art work were done by Andy Duvall. Layout was done by Lyn Chaffee. Sincere appreciation also goes to the many individuals in state offices and national organizations who helped improve this product by reviewing certain sections.

EXECUTIVE SUMMARY

Because of significant economic and social changes during the past 20 years, child care and early education issues have become a high priority in state legislatures nationwide. As more parents enter the work force—including more women and two-parent families of all income levels—state decision makers are helping them secure child care that is both affordable and supportive of their child's development. Recent scientific evidence about the brain confirms that learning begins at birth and that very young children benefit from stimulating attention with responsive caregivers, including parents and others outside the home. In the context of an increased number of working families, this research underscores the important role of a child care provider. Other studies have found that quality early care and education services have a dramatic long-term effect on a child's ability to succeed in school, achieve economically and avoid the criminal justice system. Therefore, child care and early childhood education must meet children's cognitive and emotional needs, as well as protect their physical well-being. Because several studies indicate a lack of good child care, state legislators are examining policies that can increase the availability of affordable, quality services.

Reliable, affordable care for working families clearly benefits the current work force as well, affecting economic initiatives, productivity of workers and the success of state welfare-to-work initiatives. In the wake of the federal enactment of welfare reform, most states are still in the early stages of developing systems that help families that are dependent on welfare locate stable jobs and eventually reach self-sufficiency. Child care is a crucial ingredient of these efforts.

Child care no longer is considered separate from learning. Instead, care and education are simultaneous–children learn in all settings. These include:

- Child care for infants, toddlers, preschool-age, and school-age children in centers, in family child care homes, and by relatives.
- Head Start early childhood education programs for low-income 3-, 4- and 5-year-olds.
- Prekindergarten programs, which can be school-based or community-based.
- Out-of-school time activities, including tutoring or recreation.

Recognizing the important economic and social implications of early care and education, more state legislators are adopting innovative policies that support working families' access to good care that both promotes work place effectiveness and healthy development of young children. During the last 13 years, the legislation addressing early childhood issues has grown from 28 laws in 1984 to 130 in the 1997 legislative session. A growing number of these initiatives address multiple issues that affect many components of an effective early care and education system. These comprehensive policies often connect various programs, agencies and funding sources. Increasingly, state legislatures are focusing on substantial investments in these services. In 1994, the states and the District of Columbia appropriated more than $2.4 billion for early childhood programs.

This guide closely examines the issues and tradeoffs in key child care policy decisions that face state legislators. It provides a discussion of state efforts to build supply, improve quality and develop effective subsidy systems for low-income families. By presenting research findings and policy options about supply, quality and funding for low-income child care, as well as demographic trends, this guide offers a context within which state lawmakers can have a successful, lasting effect on current and future generations.

Long-Term Effects of Early Childhood Care and Education

Good early care and education programs can provide children with a solid foundation for later success at school and at work by acting as a buffer between children and a variety of developmental risk factors. Several outcome studies have found that quality early childhood programs significantly enhance a child's educational attainment, level of socialization and long-term earning potential. These benefits translate into reduced state spending on social services and special education, increased tax revenues, a better-prepared work force and reduced crime rates. The best-known outcome study of the benefits of quality early childhood education is the High/Scope Perry Preschool Project. This study's most recent evaluation of 27-year-olds born in poverty who attended a quality preschool program at ages 3 and 4 found that participants had higher earnings, better educational achievement and fewer arrests. Other studies support these and related findings.

The first three years of life are a critical period during which the brain is creating the neural connections that support reasoning, emotion, language, motor skills, perception, values and other capacities. A child who lacks appropriate relationships and stimulation during these years will be less able to learn, cope with stress, handle emotions and form relationships. These new findings have recently been in the national spotlight. They have been covered in a prime-time network television show and at a 1997 White House conference, and have been the focus of resources from a plethora of national foundations, businesses and organizations.

It is estimated that by 2000, 70 percent of women with preschool age children will be employed and in need of child care. Many working men and women with children under age 12 experience child care breakdowns, which are linked to higher absenteeism and tardiness. Nationwide, businesses lose $3 billion annually because of child care-related absenteeism, turnover and lost productivity. Many studies have shown that reliable, high-quality care can make a decisive difference in helping families work. For low-income families that have fewer available resources, child care assistance can make the difference by allowing a parent to retain a job or leave welfare, leading to longer term benefits for a state's economy. A recent North Carolina study found that a child care subsidy that allows a parent to earn at least $15,000 per year will generate tax revenue in excess of the subsidy.

Expanding the Supply of Child Care

State legislators can increase the supply of child care by helping providers overcome the financial, legal and regulatory obstacles to starting or expanding a child care business. Some of the many supply-building options include assisting with facility development, recruiting caregivers, expanding school-age child care, establishing public and private partnerships, and changing child care liability insurance laws and local zoning ordinances. To help develop more child care facilities, at least 13 state legislatures have enacted laws that offer low-interest loans for construction or renovation of child care centers. Some states also have established loan guarantee initiatives to help child care programs afford debt. Another approach used in several states is to issue bonds and to use the proceeds to pay for early childhood facilities. At least 10 states have provided grants to child care programs to expand facilities.

Other than facility development, state policy makers often direct child care supply-building strategies to resource and referral services, which recruit providers, offer outreach to local businesses about work and family options, and educate parents about child care options. Several state and local governments also are forging partnerships with private businesses to bolster a system of resources and options for dependent care assistance for employees. Many states have adopted a range of policies to increase out-of-school time activities for school-age children. Research suggests that these programs help children increase their social skills and academic outcomes and avoid problem behaviors.

Improving the Quality of Child Care

Two national studies of child care have recently found that the majority of settings offer poor to mediocre services. The *Cost, Quality and Child Outcomes Study of Child Care Centers* revealed that 86 percent of centers studied provided mediocre to poor services and 40 percent of the infant-toddler rooms were observed to endanger children's health and safety. *The Study of Children in Family Child Care and Relative Care* found that only 9 percent of the family child care settings studied were of good quality, while 35 percent of the settings studied were so poor that they could inhibit children's development.

Across the nation, state legislators are addressing this concern through a variety of policies. One approach is to strengthen regulatory standards for child care providers. Some states encourage providers to meet additional standards such as accreditation. Licensing or regulatory standards typically address issues that have been correlated with better quality care, including child-to-staff ratios, group sizes, and training and education of caregivers and administrators. Other key regulatory issues include inspections, background checks of providers, curricula, and health and safety standards.

Another way to enhance child development is to maintain caregiver continuity for children. A key challenge for state policy makers is to reduce child care turnover rates, which are much higher than average (ranging from 35 percent to 41 percent). In addition, child care providers earn as much as $5,000 less per year than they could earn in other jobs for which they are qualified. Several state legislatures have addressed this concern by connecting provider training and education to professional advancement or to better wages and benefits. To help facilitate a career development system, all states direct funding to resource and referral programs, which can assist providers with regulatory requirements, offer training to providers at all levels and connect providers to educational resources.

Most states operate a part-day preschool program, many of which offer quality services. At least 13 states and the District of Columbia supplement the federal Head Start program for preschoolers, which includes specific quality components. States are linking their child care subsidy systems with part-day preschool programs not only to infuse quality features into the system, but also to meet the full-day needs of working parents. To promote such coordination, several states have integrated all their early childhood services into one agency or department. Similarly, a few state legislatures have restructured their committee organization to cover critical early care and education issues more comprehensively. Several states have incorporated an array of services into their child care programs that supports parents and other family members. These family support services often include health, social services, counseling, job placement services, housing, transportation, parent education or home visitation for parents with newborns. Family support programs differ in setting, format and emphasis. Some focus on a single outcome and others have broadly defined goals. They are usually in a central location, such as a public school or community agency. In addition to adding comprehensive services to an early care and education system, family support services can address multiple needs in a single place.

Child Care Funding for Children from Low-Income Families

With the federal enactment of the Personal Responsibility and Work Opportunity Reconciliation Act of 1996, states were given flexibility to design child care systems for welfare recipients, former welfare recipients in jobs, training or education and other low-income or moderate-income working families. In establishing the child care system under the federal law, states are addressing three fundamental policies: who is eligible, how much those parents will pay and what the state will reimburse providers of subsidized care. The federal law requires states to place 30 percent of its welfare recipients into job activities in fiscal year 1998 and 50 percent by 2002. Under the act, families on welfare must participate in a work-related activity within two years or less of receiving welfare. These requirements increase the pressure on states to develop a child care system that not only helps move welfare recipients into work, but that also provides child care assistance to working poor families who may need it to continue working and stay off welfare.

State decision makers are taking various approaches when choosing who should receive child care subsidies. One strategy that several states are using takes advantage of the flexibility of the new welfare law by not considering welfare status as a condition of eligibility for certain funds. Instead, these states direct available funds to any family that is below a specified income level, whether or not the family is on welfare. By guaranteeing child care services to certain families, these states effectively eliminate a waiting list. Other states maintain a child care priority for families that receive welfare or families that have recently left welfare. Another approach that some states are taking is to provide child care to families based on income categories and to make assistance available to families in a higher income category if funds are available. Under the federal law, states may exempt families with a child under age 1 from work participation requirements. In addition, states are prohibited from sanctioning nonworking welfare recipients with a child under age 6 if parents cannot locate child care that is reasonably close, affordable, suitable and appropriate. States can define these terms broadly, potentially reducing the burden on child care supply.

States have some flexibility in designing a parent fee structure, including which families pay how much of a copayment and the methods used to determine the copayment. During the past year, states developed their fee scales and legislators and administrators decided whether to exempt welfare recipients and other poor families from a copayment. Most states base the parent sliding fee scale on income levels and family size, but some states also factor the cost of care into the parent fee. This strategy may discourage eligible families with limited resources from choosing higher-cost care, which often includes higher-quality care, so this policy may have long-term effects on child development.

Another factor states are considering when examining funding issues is the level of reimbursement they pay to child care providers. Adequate reimbursement rates are critical to the effort to maintain a child care strategy that achieves both work force and child development goals, since providers are less able to afford to serve subsidized children if the reimbursement rates are too low. Some states have established differential rates that pay more to providers that meet higher regulatory standards, achieve national accreditation or serve children during nontraditional hours. These state incentives are intended to encourage better quality care and harder to find care. States also set policies regarding how subsidized care is paid for, including contracts, vouchers, cash to parents or welfare grant increases for working welfare recipients.

This guide highlights recent state legislative efforts to expand early care and education, improve the quality of services to promote healthy child development and establish effective policies to assist low-income families reach self-sufficiency. The guide includes profiles of states that have established comprehensive child care and early education policies that are often coordinated to benefit the entire family. State early childhood initiatives have a significant effect both on today's work force and on the ability of the next generation to succeed.

INTRODUCTION

The care and education of the nation's youngest children has become a critical public policy issue affecting millions of families. At the October 1997 White House Conference on Child Care, President Clinton called child care "the single most important question about social policy today."[1] Demand for child care is growing as more women with children enter the workforce, both by choice and by necessity. At the same time, researchers have discovered more about how learning begins at birth and that very young children need stimulating interaction with responsive, attentive caregivers in order to forge the neural connections that are critical to success throughout life.[2] It is now clear that child care must meet children's cognitive and emotional needs, as well as safeguard their physical well-being. Many child care settings, however, fail to provide young children with the relationships, activities and environment necessary for adequate levels of learning and development. The lack of good child care carries heavy long-term social costs in the form of higher crime rates, increases in social services spending and reduced productivity on the part of both working parents and future generations.[3] The success of states' welfare-to-work initiatives, economic initiatives and education improvement initiatives will depend in large measure on the availability of good child care.

More state legislatures are recognizing the importance of good early care and education services and are adopting innovative policies aimed at accomplishing three related goals: supporting the healthy development of all children, supporting families' access to quality care and enhancing parents' productivity, participation and stability in the workplace. Because these policies touch on a wide range of issues, they affect many state government jurisdictions (economic development, education, health, juvenile justice, welfare reform and family support). Among other things, state lawmakers are:

- Appropriating funds to help low-income families pay for child care;
- Developing innovative financing mechanisms and public-private partnerships to increase supply or improve quality;
- Ensuring that the legal framework for regulation works to prevent harm to children;
- Improving child care by, among other things, promoting stronger provider qualifications, career development and improved compensation;
- Creating incentives to encourage programs to provide higher quality care; and
- Encouraging the coordination of child care with other activities such as part-day preschool programs, Head Start, health services and family support programs.

About This Guide

This publication is intended as a practical guide for state legislators and legislative staff who are involved in making important policy decisions in the area of child care and early childhood education. It highlights the options available to policy makers, together with associated benefits, costs and tradeoffs. Examining the tradeoffs and reviewing other state experiences may help policy makers in their legislative decision making. Although this guide emphasizes state policies initiated during the past year or so, some of the policies mentioned have existed for several years.

This introduction provides a brief background about why state lawmakers should be concerned about child care issues, the increase in demand for child care services, concerns with the current supply of child care, what children and their families need from child care and the characteristics of good care. The remainder of the guide consists of four parts:

- **Expanding the supply of child care** through facilities development, public/private partnerships, loans and grants, resource and referral services, and expanding out-of-school time activities;
- **Improving the quality of child care** through regulations, accreditation and additional standards, training, career development and compensation, and quality early childhood education initiatives;
- **Funding for low-income child care**, including eligibility issues, parent fees and reimbursement rates and policies; and
- **Selected state experiences**: California, Colorado, Connecticut, Florida, Illinois, Minnesota, North Carolina, Ohio and Oregon.

Why State Legislators Are Concerned About Child Care

Good early care and education programs can have a significant, positive effect on both state economies and state spending. Such programs provide children with a solid foundation for later success in school and at work. They significantly enhance children's educational attainment, level of socialization and long-term earning potential by acting as a buffer between children and a variety of developmental risk factors. These benefits can translate into reduced state spending on social services and special education, increased tax revenues, a better prepared workforce and reduced crime rates.

Improvements in the supply and quality of child care also help families contribute more to state economies. The productivity of working parents suffers when there are problems with child care. Many families have multiple child care arrangements, which often are unreliable and unstable. One of four working mothers of a child under age 12 experienced child care breakdowns two to five times during a three-month period. These breakdowns were linked to higher absenteeism and tardiness at work.[4] According to Work/Family Directions, 83 percent of women and 71 percent of men with working wives missed work due to dependent care issues. Analysts estimate that businesses nationwide lose $3 billion every year due to child care-related absenteeism, turnover and lost productivity.[5] A child care subsidy that enables a parent in North Carolina to earn at least $15,000 per year will generate federal, state and local tax revenue in excess of the subsidy.[6]

States can improve the quality and supply of child care with carefully targeted investments of public funds in certain areas such as the education and compensation of caregivers. Investment can make a significant difference in future state costs. Recent research by the High/Scope Perry Preschool Project has determined that states can save $7.16 for every $1 spent on high-quality early childhood education services for at-risk children.[7]

The Growing Demand for Child Care

Women with young children are entering the workforce in ever-increasing numbers. Approximately 64 percent of married women with children under age 6 now work outside the home, compared with only 19 percent in 1960. It is estimated that by 2000, 70 percent of women with children under age 5 will be employed and in need of child care. Fifty-seven percent of single mothers currently are in the workforce. The increase in working women from both dual-earner and single-parent families is expected to continue well into the next century. In 1992, 75 percent of women age 25 to 54 were working. By 2005, it is projected that 83 percent of women will be in the work force.[9] The dramatic increase in the number of working mothers is attributable to several factors:

How Governments Intervene in Child Care Markets

Ideally, market forces produce what consumers need at a price they can afford. For various reasons, however, the private child care market has been unable to accomplish this goal. Good child care, particularly infant and toddler care, is simply too expensive for many families. With limited support from government and private donations, for-profit child care centers rely on parents to pay about 90 percent of their costs, while nonprofit centers use parent fees to cover about 56 percent of costs. Nevertheless, parent fees overall represent only about one-half of the amount of money required to produce good child care. The resulting market offers few choices and mediocre care.

Because of the many societal benefits associated with good child care—including higher levels of educational achievement and employment, better health, lower crime rates and reduced social services spending—state governments have an interest in remedying market failure. States have an array of policy approaches, or tools, with which to intervene in the market to increase the supply of good child care.

- *Expanding the purchasing power of consumers through subsidies (including vouchers) and tax credits;*

- *Direct provision of services, such as Head Start and public prekindergarten programs; and*

- *Linking market-based approaches with public programs, such as combining private child care with Head Start services.*

As Georgetown professor William Gormley Jr. points out, "The government's tools are no more interchangeable than, say, a hammer and a wrench."[8] These tools are, however, complementary and work well together. Therefore, states are combining various policy approaches in packages designed to meet specific needs.

- Women have wider career opportunities than ever;
- In most two-parent families, both parents work;
- A dramatic increase in the number of families headed by single mothers as a result of higher divorce rates;
- An unprecedented number of women formerly on welfare are entering the workforce; and
- A growing use of early care and education programs by parents who are seeking an enriched experience for their children.[10]

In the wake of these demographic shifts, the percentage of children in child care centers and preschools increased from 23 percent in 1991 to 30 percent in 1993.[11] In a recent study, 62 percent of families identified locating quality child care services as their most significant work and family problem.[12]

Child Care for Low-Income Families

Families often have difficulty locating child care that is good, reliable and affordable. It is especially difficult to find care for infants and toddlers (who are in critical periods of brain development) and care for school-age children. The shortage of good, affordable care affects families at all income levels. Child care, even mediocre care, is expensive for an individual family. It has been estimated that the average American family spends between $4,000 and $10,000 per year for the care of a single child. This is equal to what families pay for college tuition plus room and board at a public university. The cost of care, however, varies depending on region, type of care and age of the child. In Boston, for example, care for one 3-year-old costs approximately $8,840 per year and infant and toddler care costs even more.[16] The lack of affordable care is especially hard on low-income families. The U.S. Census Bureau reported that families earning less than $1,200 per month who pay for care spend 25 percent of their income on child care, compared to 6 percent for an upper income family.[17] Nearly 25 percent of all infants, toddlers and preschoolers in the United States are members of low-income families.[18] Figure 1 shows the disproportionate share of income that poor families pay for child care.

What Is Child Care?

As used in this publication, the term "child care" means all types of education and care for children from birth through age 5 and programs for school-age children before and after school and during vacations. It refers to a wide range of programs located in different types of facilities, under a variety of auspices, and with different hours of operation, from part-day to full-day (see figure 2).

Child care no longer is considered separate from learning. Instead, care and education of young children are simultaneous—children learn in all settings. High-quality programs address two policy objectives. They provide safe environments that allow parents to work without worrying about their children. At the same time, these programs can provide stimulating and nurturing settings that foster healthy child development, prepare children to succeed in school and give them the tools they need to develop into productive adults.[13]

Examples of child care are:

- *Care for infants, toddlers, preschool and school-age children provided in child care centers, in family child care homes and by relatives.*
- *Center child care is provided under public and private sponsorship by for-profit and nonprofit organizations. Today, there are approximately 90,000 centers in the United States, including 6,000 owned by for-profit chains, 29,000 independent for-profit centers, 25,000 independent nonprofit centers, 15,000 church-based centers and 8,000 others sponsored by nonprofit organizations.[14]*
- *Family child care providers generally are sole proprietors of an in-home business who provide care for children from infancy through age 12.*
- *Relative care is child care by relatives other than the child's parent.*
- *Head Start programs that offer a comprehensive array of social services to low-income children and their families in addition to providing early childhood education services. Most Head Start programs operate for only a few hours a day or only a few days a week.*
- *Prekindergarten programs, which typically target children from low-income families and provide early childhood education services during the school year. Most of these programs are part-day, but some are full-day. These programs traditionally are operated by local school districts, although some states permit schools to contract with a Head Start or other community-based child care program to provide services either in or near the school.*
- *Out-of-school time activities, including tutoring and recreation, for children age 5 and older in public elementary or middle schools or other facilities such as YMCAs. In 1991, 1.7 million children from kindergarten through eighth grade attended 49,500 school-age programs. At the same time, however, the Census Bureau estimates that about 4.6 million children are in self-care, which is defined as being alone 25 hours or more weekly.[15]*

Besides the problem of affordability, child care, preschool and other programs—especially subsidized care—are less likely to be available in poorer communities. Just a few years ago, 36 states (or three out of four) had child care waiting lists for eligible low-income children, illustrating the need for more subsidized care.[19] The U.S. General Accounting Office has reported that only 35 percent of poor 3- and 4-year-olds participate in preschool, compared with more than 60 percent of the highest income 3- and 4-year-olds.[20] A recent study of three communities found that 54 percent of school-age children from low-income families were not enrolled in after-school programs because of problems with cost, transportation, safety and other considerations.[21] Due to access problems, and for other reasons, many low-income families choose relative care. Middle-income working families also struggle to locate affordable care and generally are not eligible for a child care subsidy.[22]

Although the number of child care centers has increased nearly 300 percent since the late 1960s, a 1995 national study found that 86 percent of today's centers offer only mediocre or poor quality services.[23] A Families and Work Institute study of family child care found that only 9 percent of providers offered good quality care and that the care provided in 35 percent of

Figure 1.   Percent of Monthly Family Income Spent on Child Care by Family Income and Poverty Status*

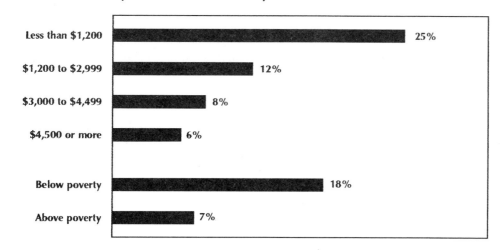

*Limited to families with a preschooler.

Source: Lynne Casper's *What Does It Cost to Mind Our Preschoolers?* Based on the *Survey of Income and Program Participation*, U.S. Census Bureau report.

Figure 2.   Care Arrangements Used by Families With Employed Mothers for Preschoolers: 1993

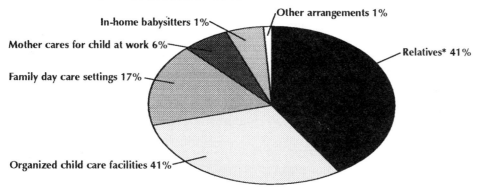

*Includes fathers, siblings grandparents and other relatives.

Source: Lynne Casper's *What Does It Cost to Mind Our Preschoolers?* Based on the *Survey of Income and Program Participation*, U.S. Census Bureau report.

family child care homes was actually growth-harming.[24] Mediocre and harmful care is characterized by high worker turnover resulting in frequent disruptions in the relationship between child and caregiver, a lack of responsive interaction between caregivers and children, lax health and safety practices, poorly trained staff and lack of parental involvement.

What Children and Their Families Need from Child Care

The first three years of life are a critical period during which the brain is creating the neural connections that support reasoning, emotion, language, motor skills, perception, values and other capacities. Children develop all these capacities at the same time through experiences.

Turnover of Child Care Staff Is a Major Concern

As a result of low wages, staff turnover in the child care industry is extremely high. The turnover rate for all child care staff ranges from about 33 percent to 41 percent, according to various reports. This rate is approximately four times the annual rate of 9.6 percent reported by all U.S. companies in 1992 and three times the annual rate of 12 percent reported by non-business companies, such as government, schools, and other nonprofit organizations.[25] Turnover of teachers in child care settings nearly tripled between the mid-1970s and 1990.[26] Staff turnover is harmful to children, who become attached to their caregivers and depend on consistent relationships for the development of learning, trust and self-esteem. The high turnover problem is largely the result of low wages and poor benefits. Child care providers earn as much as $5,000 less per year than they could earn in other jobs for which they are qualified.[27] A national wage study found that most child care workers earn $12,058 per year (slightly above minimum wage) and receive no benefits or paid leave. Family child care providers earn an average of $9,528 annually after expenses.[28]

Nurturing and responsive relationships during this period are crucial to the brain's development of cognition and social development. As a child interacts with the world, the number of neural connections within his or her brain soars. A child who lacks appropriate relationships and stimulation during the first three years of life will be less able to learn, cope with stress, handle emotions and form relationships.

To reach positive outcomes, child care should provide children with an environment that meets children's need for relationships, nurture and interaction. In particular, children need a safe, healthy physical environment and consistent relationships with caregivers who are:

- attentive and responsive to children and who engage them in stimulating activities;
- trained in the area of child development;
- in frequent contact with parents; and
- respectful and supportive of the family's cultural values and traditions.

Child care should meet the needs of parents as well as their children. Parents, of course, want what is best for their children, namely skilled caregivers who demonstrate warmth and interest in their child, a rich environment for learning, and the opportunity to talk and share information with caregivers. Parents also need good child care that is:

- available during work or school hours, including nontraditional hours such as nights or on weekends;
- reasonably close to home, school or work;
- reliable, so that disruptions to work or school are kept to a minimum; and
- affordable.

Characteristics of Good Child Care Programs

Analysts have identified several key measures by which to evaluate the quality of child care programs:

- Low numbers of children per staff;
- Low numbers of children in a single group;
- Adequate staff training and higher education in child development;
- Adequate staff compensation; and
- Sufficient experience of supervisory personnel.

Although researchers and advocates have determined what constitutes good child care, it is up to policy makers, including state legislators, to ensure that good care is available to those who need it. Legislators can play a central role in improving services to support working families and their children. One report suggests that five key elements make up a child care infrastructure:

- **Parent information and education** about child care options and characteristics of quality care.
- **Professional development and credentialing**, including training, licensing, education, career development and professional support.
- **Facility licensing**, including a system to ensure that child care facilities promote learning, health and safety.
- **Funding** to ensure that all families have access to good child care.
- **Governance,** including the means for planning, data collection, information sharing and monitoring accountability.[29]

EXPANDING THE SUPPLY OF CHILD CARE

State legislators can increase the supply of child care by helping providers overcome the financial, legal and regulatory obstacles to starting or expanding a child care business. This section discusses the following strategies for expanding the supply of child care:

- Financial assistance for facilities development
- Resource and referral services
- Strategies for expanding school-age child care
- Public and private partnerships
- Other initiatives

Facilities Development

The cost of constructing child care centers is high. The General Services Administration found that the child care centers in 100 federal office buildings cost 43 percent more to construct than the other parts of the buildings.[30] As a result of the high cost of construction, child care centers often are located in underutilized storefronts, publicly owned community centers and surplus public properties. Child care centers are provided in various types of facilities, including those owned, leased or rented by nonprofit and for-profit groups, and in no- or low-cost space such as space donated by a church or in a public school. A national study of 400 centers found that almost two-thirds of the 200 nonprofit centers studied incurred little or no cost for facilities as result of donations. About one-tenth of the for-profit centers had low- or no-cost facilities.[31]

Although reduced facility costs help to lower the cost of child care to consumers, child care providers still face high operating costs, due primarily to the cost of personnel.[32] Operating costs other than personnel costs sometimes are donated or made available at a reduced price to nonprofit child care agencies.

State decision making in the area of facility development is based on an analysis of the child care market, economic conditions, and available state and community resources. Policies can be targeted to create facilities for specific consumer groups such as low-income families or to specific types of care that may not be readily available, such as infant and toddler care. Legislators will want to consider several questions related to facility development, including:

- Where is the need for facilities? Are there specific types of care or groups of working families in need of facilities to house child care services?
- How will the facility development program be financed? Will a grant, loan, or tax abatement program include all providers in the child care market (family child care, nonprofit centers, and public agencies)? Also, how will the program be marketed to promote access to funds for all sectors and in all targeted areas?

8

- What is the expected effect of the program on the current market of providers, both private and public?
- How will the loan program be funded (through a bond issue, state funds or state financial institutions)? Should the state guarantee the loans?
- How will the program be administered in state government?
- How will the new program meet its annual operating budget?
- How will the program be linked to other financing opportunities for center development?

State loans and grants for facility development, which generally range from $10,000 to $30,000, usually are inadequate to cover the cost of constructing or renovating new centers. Therefore, child care organizations that want to build or modify a center need to develop a financial package, including funds from both public and private sources. In addition to grants and loans, states can assist child care administrators to negotiate financing for facility development. In some communities, such technical assistance is available through intermediary organizations such as a community development organization or a resource and referral program.[33] State legislators can promote the development of low- or no-cost facilities by means of the following strategies:

- Direct loans
- Loan guarantees
- Grants
- Bond issues

States also provide tax credits for facility development as well as other child care expenses. Tax credits are discussed in the section on private and public partnerships.

Direct Loan Programs
At least 13 states have established direct loan programs to increase the supply of facilities.[34] Loans are a relatively low-cost way to provide the development of child care facilities because state costs generally are limited to administration and marketing.

- *Maryland's* Child Care Facilities Direct Loan Fund finances up to 50 percent of the cost of construction, renovation or acquisition of real property for the expansion or development of a child care facility. Administered by the state Department of Business and Economic Development, the program has financed 36 loans since 1988 totaling $4.5 million to facilities that serve 4,174 children. Using federal Child Care and Development Block Grant (CCDBG) funds, Maryland also has a Child Care Special Loan Fund that provides direct loans of up to $10,000 to upgrade facilities or purchase items for them. Ninety-one projects have received financing totaling more than $467,000.
- *Ohio's* Day Care Grant and Loan Program established a revolving loan fund that makes micro-loans of up to $25,000 to start or expand family child care homes or centers.
- *Connecticut's* 1997 school readiness bill requires low-interest loans for construction or renovation of a range of facilities for early childhood programs. It establishes a quasi-public agency to coordinate child care financing and requires a priority for accredited programs with a school readiness plan and for those promoting co-location. The state facilities plan is mandated to include facilities that provide full-day, year-round programs, accredited programs, and those integrated with school readiness programs.[35]

Loan Guarantee Programs
In addition to direct loans, some states have loan guarantee programs, which are an inexpensive way to help child care programs that can afford debt build facilities. Administration of loan guarantee programs can be relatively simple, and intermediary organizations can provide technical assistance to child care centers that are inexperienced with capital financing.[36]

Maryland was one of the first states to develop a loan guarantee program. Maryland established the Day Care Facilities Loan Guarantee Fund in 1984, which has guaranteed 62 loans totaling $8.9 million that created 4,273 child care slots. Based on the success of the loan guarantee program, *Maryland* established the direct loan program described above. *Arkansas, California, Connecticut, New York, North Carolina,* and *Tennessee* are among the states that also have enacted loan guarantee programs.[37]

Bond Issues

Some states have used the proceeds from the sale of bonds as a source of funds for the development of child care facilities. *Minnesota* issued general obligation bonds in 1992, 1994 and 1996 and used the proceeds to pay for early care and education facilities owned by public entities to house Head Start and early childhood special education programs. In *Illinois*, the Illinois Facilities Fund (IFF) used tax-exempt bonds to construct and renovate child care centers. The IFF acts as the intermediary between the bond issuing authority and the child care development project. The fund has financed more than $15 million in facilities construction during the past 10 years, creating spaces for 1,700 children in approximately 30 centers. *Hawaii* also issues tax-exempt bonds for the development and renovation of child care facilities.[38]

Facilities Grant Programs

At least 10 states have established grant programs to expand the availability of child care facilities.[39] Some states administer their own grant programs, while others delegate administration to community-based nonprofit intermediary organizations such as community development institutions, economic development corporations, and resource and referral or human services organizations.

Creating a grant program depends on available resources, state priorities and need. As with loan programs, state lawmakers set priorities for grants, including:

- the development of facilities for services to meet the need for specific types of care and
- the development of facilities for underserved populations of working families.

State grants can be used to renovate or expand existing facilities. Grants also can be used to modify buildings to serve special populations or to meet state regulations.

- *Maryland's* Family Day Care Provider Grant Fund, established in 1988, reimburses providers up to $500 for expenses incurred in meeting state and local regulations, including expenses associated with modifying facilities.
- *New Jersey* provides technical assistance and small grants to applicants that either start or expand a child care center for 10 to 35 children. Both established and newly developed facilities are eligible for assistance.
- *California* legislators initiated a program under which the state purchases portable buildings and leases them to early childhood programs. The state's $25 million revolving loan fund is primarily used for this program.[40]

Resource and Referral Services (R&Rs)

Although they generally do not provide direct services for children and families, R&Rs help build supply and ensure more efficient use of existing child care resources by educating parents at all income levels regarding their child care options; recruiting providers to fill gaps in service, such as infant care; providing outreach to local businesses about work and family options; and finding substitute care for family child care.

R&Rs also promote quality services. These issues and state examples are discussed further on p. 22.

Strategies to Expand the Supply of School-Age Child Care

States have adopted a variety of policies to increase the supply of care for children ages 5 to 12 when they are not in school. All the policies require careful collaboration between school districts and child care providers. These services often are referred to as "out-of-school time" services and apply to both elementary and middle school students. These policies include:

- Targeting state funds for out-of-school time programs;
- Promoting school-age child care in the public schools;
- Avoiding unnecessary regulation of specialized recreation programs; and
- Allowing school buses to be used to transport children from school to child care.

Some examples of state strategies to expand out-of-school time programs include the following:

- In FY 1997, *Hawaii* invested $15 million in its A+ Program, which provides after-school care to children in kindergarten to sixth grade.
- *California* spends nearly $26 million for its extended day program direct services. The state has invested in the program since 1985. In addition, as part of a larger bond act in 1996, voters approved $5 million in bond funds for school-age care facilities.
- In its Education Reform Act of 1990, *Kentucky* created a statewide network of family resource and youth centers in schools that serve at-risk children. These centers offer a wide range of services, including after-school, before-school and summer child care in areas where school-age child care is unavailable.
- The *Georgia* School Age Care Association (GSACA) initiated the 3:00 Project, which offers out-of-school activities to middle-school children in the areas of community service learning, academic enrichment, socialization and recreation, and communication strategies. The project serves about 1,000 children at 17 sites throughout the state and is funded through a public/private partnership among the state General Assembly and several nonprofit organizations, including four private foundations. The GSACA also created a School Age and Youth Certificate Program and was instrumental in the decision to reserve 50 percent of Child Care and Development Block Grant quality funds for out-of-school programs; this represents one of the highest percentages in the country.
- *Alabama* rapidly expanded school-based programs through a carefully designed competitive grant program that requires local school systems to create partnerships and coordinate existing services. The initiative also requires the involvement of parents on local extended day advisory councils. In addition to grant funds, the state Department of Education provides technical assistance and training to schools. The program currently serves more than 16,000 children daily in extended day programs.
- *New Hampshire* created a private, nonprofit agency called PlusTime NH to educate business, religious and community leaders about the importance of school-age child care and to generate funding and public support for expansion of out-of-school programs. The state attributes the success of PlusTime NH to its diverse board of directors, which includes representatives from child care providers, charitable organizations, businesses, churches, health care providers, school districts and child advocacy groups.[41]

Public and Private Sector Partnerships

States are finding that public and private partnerships are one way to expand the supply of good child care services. Employers benefit when their employees' children are in stable, reliable care. Nevertheless, in 1996, only about 1 percent of child care funding came from businesses.[42] This section highlights efforts to increase the involvement of employers in child care. State approaches have included:

- Statewide business commissions to examine financing and make recommendations;

- Local planning councils to involve businesses in child care funding;
- Tax credits to encourage businesses to become involved in the development of child care facilities and to assist employees with child care costs;
- Public service announcements; and
- Community funds in which businesses may invest.

Public and Private Partnerships—Selected Strategies

- *Florida* established a state executive partnership to encourage local, employer and foundation support for child care for working families. The state's 1996 welfare reform law established a public-private partnership to fund child care subsidies to low-income working families. The Legislature appropriated $2 million to be matched by $2 million from businesses. Employers met the match and the Legislature doubled the state's share to $4 million in 1997. *Florida* also recognizes family-friendly employers through a program of awards and positive publicity.

- Seventeen *Indiana* counties participate in the Indiana Symposium on Child Care Financing. The symposium's goal in 1995 was to encourage private sector employers to become leaders on child care issues and to invest in improving the supply and quality of child care. As a result of the work of the symposium, the Indiana Donors Alliance, representing 70 community foundations, has agreed to house the Indiana Child Care Fund, which will raise corporate, foundation and individual contributions to improve child care throughout the state.

- *Colorado* established a Business Commission on Child Care Financing. Chaired by a bank president, the commission examined ways the state could expand and finance good child care. The commission recommended resource guides for businesses and consumers, a multi-bank community development corporation to provide loans and other financial assistance to child care providers, a child care check-off on state income tax returns, a child care income tax credit, a governor's statewide summit on business and child care, and policies to allow the use of public educational buildings for school-age child care.

- *Hawaii* created a nonprofit corporation governed by representatives from state government, businesses and foundations.

- *New Jersey* developed an employer approach to support parents with young children by providing partial wage replacement for parental leave through its temporary disability insurance (TDI) program. When combined with accumulated vacation and sick leave, this benefit can be an important source of support for working mothers because they can remain at home with their child during early infancy. Four other states—*California, Rhode Island, New York, and Hawaii*—and *Puerto Rico* also have TDI programs.

- *The Allegheny County Early Childhood Initiative, located in* Allegheny County, Pennsylvania, with the United Way and the philanthropic community is seeking funds for quality child care and education services for low-income children in the community. United Way is leading the campaign to raise $59 million from the private sector. Local businesses that contribute are asked to play a public advocacy role and to assist in public development efforts. After five years, government will replace private seed money with public funds. In this initiative, early childhood professionals set high standards for programs, and neighborhood groups design services to reflect local values.

- *The American Business Collaborative* (ABC) brings together more than 80 companies, including some of the nation's largest, to increase the supply and quality of dependent care services. From 1992 through 1994, the collaborative invested more than $27 million in a range of grants for child and elder care activities. About 50 percent of the funds were granted to early care and education programs, about 38 percent to school-age care and about 12 percent to elder care. Now in phase two, the ABC has committed to spend $100 million in a six-year initiative to increase its emphasis on quality improvement and to continue its strategy of planning at the community level.[43]

Employer Tax Incentives—State Initiatives
At least 18 states have enacted corporate tax credits or deductions to encourage businesses to give their employees more child care options.[44]

- *Arkansas* lawmakers established several tax incentives for companies that create or operate child care facilities. Companies can receive a corporate tax credit of 3.9 percent on the salaries of employees who work at child care facilities and are exempt from sales and use taxes for building construction and furnishings.
- *California* has a corporate tax credit for child care start-up costs, information and referral services, child care facility construction costs and contributions to a qualified care plan.
- *Connecticut* authorized a tax credit equal to 40 percent of the cost of providing parent education classes to employees, available once the state's employer child care tax credit is exhausted. Classes must provide certain child development information and referrals.
- *Florida* corporations may deduct 100 percent of the start-up costs of an on-site facility.
- *Maryland* established a child care tax credit for employers that hire welfare recipients. The tax credit ranges from 10 percent to 30 percent of wages and from $400 to $600 in child care costs. Maryland also has expanded tax credit legislation to a broader child care market with a law that exempts certain in-home family day care providers from local personal property taxes.
- *Oregon* created a 50 percent tax credit for corporations that provide funds for child care services. Under the flexible tax credit plan, employees select their provider, and corporations are allowed a credit of up to $2,500 per full-time employee.
- In *Rhode Island,* businesses with child care centers for employees must accept state-subsidized children in order to be eligible for the child care tax credit.[45]

Some surveys indicate that these tax credits are not being widely used and, therefore, have a minimal effect on the availability of child care. The possible reasons for underuse of tax credits are many, including:

- Credits do not benefit the many businesses that have no state tax liability.
- Tax credit programs have not been widely publicized in some cases.
- Employers may not trust the government's commitment to tax relief.
- Employers may have past experience with government "red tape."
- Tax incentives may not be relevant to the motivation of businesses' Human Resource decision makers.
- High administrative costs of using tax credits.
- Tax credits often are available only for child care center start-up costs, not for operating costs.[46]

Although tax credits involve some revenue loss, underuse has limited such losses in most states. In Arizona, for example, fewer than 10 corporations have taken advantage of the credit in one year. Approximate revenue loss in other states is approximately:

- Illinois: under $1 million in 1993;
- Oregon: $1 million in 1996-97;
- Montana: under $100,000 in 1993; and
- California: approximately $14 million in 1994.[47]

Other Initiatives

Other state initiatives to expand supply of child care include the following.

Changing or preempting local zoning laws

These changes can allow more family child care homes in residential areas. This strategy requires cooperation and communication between state and local government entities. *New York* successfully sued local zoning officials to establish that the state's goal of increasing the supply of child care took precedence over zoning ordinances.[48]

Assistance with obtaining or maintaining liability insurance

A recent *Oregon* law prohibits insurance companies from canceling or refusing to renew a liability policy solely because the policyholder operates a family child care home.[49]

Reforming the regulatory process

Options include:

- Consolidating and streamlining inspections by multiple agencies;
- Eliminating rules that are not necessary to reduce safety and health risks;
- Increasing licensing staff to cut down on start-up delays; and
- Increasing authorized capacity of child care homes for school-age children. This involves a trade-off between increased supply and better child-to-staff ratios, which are associated with higher quality.

IMPROVING THE QUALITY OF CHILD CARE

Several national studies of child care have found that the majority of settings studied offer poor to mediocre services. *The Cost, Quality and Child Outcomes Study of Child Care Centers* found that 86 percent of centers studied were providing mediocre to poor services. Forty percent of the infant-toddler rooms were observed to endanger children's health and safety.[50] Low quality services included health and safety problems, and low or mediocre services failed to provide the kinds of learning experiences that foster young children's development and prepare them for primary school. The Families and Work Institute found that only 9 percent of the family child care settings studied were of good quality, while 35 percent of the settings studied were so poor that they could inhibit children's development.[51]

Positive outcomes for children rely on maintaining a quality level that supports children's brain development and learning and enables them to advance from early care and education settings to kindergarten—ready to learn. Recent scientific evidence shows that a young child's brain develops a complex circuitry for language, thinking, and social skills more rapidly than previously believed.[52] This new information indicates that early childhood experiences—such as nurturing, stimulating child care with a consistent caregiver—can support healthy brain development. Specific legislative strategies that advance these quality experiences are discussed in this section. They include the following.

- **Standards and Regulations.** State legislators can set standards for child care regulation and also can encourage providers to meet additional standards. Research has correlated better regulated programs with better quality care in both centers and homes.[53]
- **Provider Training and Career Development.** A provider's education level and specific training in early care and education are related to quality.[54] These activities are part of state systems for provider career development.
- **Wages and Benefits for Providers.** Better quality programs pay providers higher wages and are more likely to offer a compensation package that includes benefits.[55] Some state initiatives pay higher rates for higher levels of quality and increased revenues can be used to support improved quality, including improved compensation.
- **Resource and Referral Services.** Many states coordinate with these programs to improve services in several ways, including training, technical assistance and regulatory assistance.
- **Preschool and Head Start.** Some state initiatives integrate early education, part-day preschool programs and child care services. This approach can both improve child care services and also better serve working families who need full-day early childhood services.
- **Adding Comprehensive Services.** Some states are supplementing child care with comprehensive health and social services to make these resources more accessible for families. Systematic approaches often are referred to as family support services.

Standards and Regulations

Child Care Regulations
State government is responsible for regulating child care centers and family child care homes.

Although the scope of regulated programs varies among the states and within provider groups, certain issues are consistently addressed in state regulation. This includes setting standards for many areas, including child-to-staff ratios, group sizes, training and education requirements for providers, health and safety, background checks, inspections and monitoring, curricula, furnishings, immunizations and smoking policies. The licensing or regulatory requirements represent the state's minimal standards to protect children's health and safety.

Regulatory policy involves tradeoffs. More stringent regulations have been found to reduce the risk of harm and help foster positive effects on children.[56] If a proposed stricter standard is not currently being widely met, enforcing it might increase costs, thereby reducing the supply of affordable care. On the other hand, less stringent regulations may result not only in a plentiful supply of unqualified care, but also in an unreliable service that consumers may fear. Somewhere between these extremes, states set their rules. Some rules affect costs more than others. The child-to-staff ratio, for example, has a significant effect on cost and quality. When states establish a rule, they can examine the number of programs that already meet it to better estimate the effect on costs.

States monitor and modify their regulations to ensure that they are effective and cost efficient. Ongoing state legislative oversight reflects state efforts to tailor regulatory systems to meet current and changing state needs and to reflect an increased understanding about children's development and the needs of working families. New knowledge about the importance of a child's early development as a foundation for later life and about the long-term outcomes of good early childhood programs has shaped the regulatory process and has expanded the use of additional standards such as accreditation.

Scope of Regulation
All 50 states license child care centers and at least some sizes of family child care homes. A few states use a form of regulation called registration—which is usually less strict than licensing—for family child care settings. Some states exempt certain early childhood programs from regulation. These typically are care by public and private elementary school systems, programs with parents on the premises and recreation programs. Public programs in schools usually are unlicensed, although a few states have begun to license preschools and other state laws require the Department of Education to set standards "no less stringent" than those of licensing. Some states have a process for preschool accreditation by the Department of Education. States generally do not require parental care or relative care to be regulated and seven states exempt religiously-operated centers from regulation (at least two other states regulate religious care only under certain circumstances).[57]

Inspections and Enforcement
States maintain regulatory compliance in three ways:

* Routine inspections,
* Technical assistance, and
* Investigation of complaints.

The licensing record, if available to parents, contains information about what rules are being met and what complaints have been investigated. These inspections are important for achieving compliance, even for centers that have achieved accreditation under a national system. A number of states have eliminated the license renewal process, instead granting an "evergreen" license, which allows states to concentrate on visiting to maintain compliance.[58] Usually, if a program willfully, repeatedly and intentionally fails to meet the rules, its license will be removed, but licensers make efforts to help programs comply before taking such an action.

Inspections are an ongoing part of the process of facilitating the development of good programs for families. Some states are trying new approaches and others are adding staff as a strategy to improve quality.

- In 1996 *Colorado* lawmakers focused licensing activities and resources on child care facilities that have demonstrated a higher risk for children in their care. Other states schedule inspections for all centers at regular intervals.
- In the 1997 session, the *Oklahoma* Legislature added 37 licensing staff to improve monitoring of programs, including programs that meet higher quality criteria in areas such as director's training, teacher qualifications, staff compensation and parent involvement.
- As a way to provide state legislative oversight, a 1997 *Connecticut* law requires an evaluation of licensed centers, including a longitudinal study of the children served.
- A 1997 *Texas* law requires a coordinated inspection system for child care facilities. This includes a computerized database to be shared among providers and authorization to release the records to the public to enhance parental choice.
- To improve the efficiency of child care monitoring, several states use a license indicator system that has saved the amount of license reviews by 50 percent to 60 percent. Under this system, a state inspector checks key licensing regulations of child care providers that have good compliance histories. These key regulations usually represent about 10 percent of all a state's child care regulations.[59]

Child-to-Staff Ratios

Research has found that good child care programs have more adults available in their classrooms for the children in care.[60] The required ratio of adults to children in child care and education settings is set by state regulation. As with other regulations, improving child-to-staff ratios can be costly to providers and some legislatures have appropriated funds for such costs. *North Carolina,* for example, spent $3.6 million during a two-year period to improve ratios in 1993 and 1994.[61] One state experience demonstrates that improving child-to-staff ratios can make a difference in the level of quality available to children. In 1991, the *Florida* Legislature changed child care child-to-staff ratios for children from infancy to three years. A study of the effect of the changes showed that, in the classrooms with the improved ratios, children's intellectual and emotional development were improved and that teachers were more sensitive and responsive to children.[62]

Staff Screening and Background Checks

To protect children in child care from abuse, exploitation and abduction, state legislatures have required staff screening and background checks. In July 1995, 47 states required criminal history checks for employees in licensed child care centers and family child care homes.[63] There are several policy questions legislators may want to consider regarding these background checks.

- Who pays for the background check? Is it the state, the provider or the prospective employee?
- Who must be checked? For instance, are all adults who are regularly on the premises of the center, home or preschool required to be checked? Are some adults or family members (in family child care) exempt?
- Will the state allow a prospective employee to work while the background check is being completed?

State experience has shown that the costs of these background checks, along with processing time, present concerns for child care providers. Costs of the background checks can be prohibitive, and staff may not be available for employment soon enough if background checks take months to be processed. Some states found they could reduce the time by assigning the task to the licensing staff, rather than to the criminal justice agency staff.[64] Legislators are continuing to enact laws to clarify background checking procedures, including cost-effective processes, and to respond to high turnover rates among child care staff.

- An *Arkansas* statute specifies procedures for background checks, allows for conditional employment during the check period, makes the provision of false information a misdemeanor, and clarifies that the employer is not liable for an employee's giving false information.
- The *California* Trustline is a registry that lists license-exempt child care providers that have cleared criminal and registry background checks. The Trustline checks in-home providers, an important service for parents who use that type of care. The registry eliminates a provider's expense for providers of repeated background checks. It also makes the list of providers more accessible for hiring.
- A 1997 *Oregon* law established a two-year criminal history registry to use for checking child care providers and applicants.[65]

Many states prohibit anyone from providing early childhood services who has committed a crime against children or has been denied an early childhood license because of abuse and neglect.

Accreditation and Additional Standards
Establishing and monitoring regulations for child care can contribute to better child care and to a parent's peace of mind. By meeting additional standards, center and in-home providers go beyond the baseline required by regulation. Studies have found that early childhood programs with certain additional standards can contribute to better outcomes.[66]

Accreditation
Accreditation for early care and education programs by the National Association for the Education of Young Children (NAEYC) is a standard for good practice.[67] Some state legislation specifically mentions NAEYC accreditation as an additional standard for programs to meet for certain purposes—a condition to receive state funds. (See "Linking Funding to Higher Standards" at the bottom of this page.) This accreditation system uses a program self-assessment followed by a validation visit from a visitor to assess a child care center's practice according to a set of criteria for the children's program, the facility, administration, staff qualifications and programs for parents. Accreditation for family child care homes also is available through the National Association of Family Child Care.

Besides tying accreditation to funding, some states give special designation to programs that meet higher standards. *Florida's* Gold Seal program is one example.[68] (See the Florida state experience section on pp. 54–56.) *North Carolina* will issue a permanent rated license to reflect program standards, provider education, and compliance history.[69]

Head Start Performance Standards
The Head Start performance standards are a set of comprehensive program guidelines required in federally-sponsored Head Start preschool programs. By following the performance standards, centers and family child care providers may improve their services. Standards include children's educational services, health policies and practice, family involvement, and administration. Some states also are directing their prekindergarten and Head Start funding to early childhood education programs that meet Head Start performance standards. (See the Head Start section on pp. 23–24 and the state experiences section on pp. 46–70.)

Linking Funding to Higher Standards
Child care centers and other early childhood programs may voluntarily meet more stringent standards as a condition of participation in a state early childhood contract, grant or initiative

that requires compliance with higher standards. Some observers refer to these as "funding standards." Because the overall quality of child care services is so low, families are likely to have difficulty finding and purchasing good care for their children.[70] This often is true for low-income children, because many of them are in care that fails to promote healthy development. One multi-state study indicates that three of every four low-income children have unsafe and unresponsive family or relative care.[71]

State Approaches
State strategies to use higher standards to improve service quality for low-income children include:

• Linking higher standards, such as accreditation, to higher reimbursement rates;
• Using tiered levels of regulatory standards to set differential reimbursement rates (see the differential reimbursement rates section on pp. 43–44);
• Contracting only with programs that meet higher standards (see the California state experience section on p. 47); and
• Purchasing services from preschool programs that follow Head Start performance standards.

A Director's Credential
Some states are beginning to develop additional training opportunities for early childhood program administrators as a way providing good services to families. Research has found that programs that provide better child care services have more experienced administrators in management positions.[72] Within the early childhood profession, professional organizations and individuals are investigating the possibility of developing a director credential. This credential would be similar to a school principal license, but it would be voluntary. Several states have begun to require specialized training for early care and education directors.[73]

• As part of the regulatory process, *California* now requires a site supervisor or a program director permit for administrators of early care and education programs.
• *Alabama, California, Massachusetts,* and *Texas* require management training, and *Texas* requires a director credential.[74]

Other states are investigating director management training through work in their career development task force or through higher education.

Provider Training and Career Development

Children's development is nurtured and enhanced when their early childhood teachers and other providers have been professionally prepared. Research has found that child care providers who have participated in early childhood training and attended courses in higher education settings are more nurturing and provide their students with more learning experiences and more interactions.[75] A young child's caregiver or teacher plays an important role in the child's development during the infant, toddler and preschool years because, as recent research indicates, a child's development, including brain development, is rapid and far-reaching during early childhood.[76] When children establish secure, ongoing attachments to trained teachers in child care settings, they are more ready for school.[77] State policy makers are investing in professional development activities for providers as a strategy for improving child care services.

Professional development activities include both higher education and various early childhood training sessions. Early childhood training includes all professional education sessions, workshops, seminars and other experiences focused on child development, teaching or other aspects of operating an early childhood program. State legislators have several policy options including:

- Mandating training for providers;
- Involving resource and referral services in training and education of providers;
- Providing compensatory incentives for training, whether mandated or voluntary; and
- Rewarding facilities that have better trained or educated staff by giving them a higher reimbursement rate. (See the differential reimbursement rates section on pp. 43–44).

Promoting professional learning activities for early childhood providers can pay off in the long term because both early childhood training and higher education have been shown to improve providers' work with children, leading to better future outcomes.[78]

State Actions To Design a Career Development System

State legislatures are participating in activities designed to create professional development opportunities for early childhood providers. These opportunities range from workshops and seminars to a statewide career development system. About two-thirds of local child care resource and referral programs are involved with higher education for provider credit and in helping providers acquire credentials through training.[79]

Key Characteristics of Effective Career Development Initiatives

- *One coordinated system for all levels of providers in all types of care. These include teachers, supervisors, directors and staff in all early childhood learning environments—schools, child care centers, Head Start programs, family child care homes, parent education and support programs.*
- *Articulation of a core body of knowledge for early childhood practitioners in all settings.*
- *A sequential system of teacher preparation and continuing staff development.*
- *Linking training and compensation.*
- *A quality control system.*
- *A system for assessing training needs, and offering training based on those needs.*
- *A system for making information about training—and the training itself—easily accessible to a wide range of teachers, supervisors, directors, and staff.*[80]

Colorado has proposed a model early childhood professional credentialing system. Components include coordination of training in higher education, noncredited training approval, learning clusters and encouragement of business investment in child care.[81] For more details, see the Colorado state experience section on p. 50.

New York has combined resources from state government, philanthropy and community agencies in an effort to plan and establish an early care and education professional career development process that includes several levels of credentialing. In the 1997 legislative session, New York lawmakers directed grant funds to this process.[82]

Targeted Training

Some state legislation prioritizes training strategies that have been shown to improve good early care and education services. These states often target allocated funds to certain provider groups, such as relative caregivers, infant and toddler teachers, administrators and family child care providers.

- *Connecticut's* 1997 school readiness law invests in a statewide career development system (described on p. 53 in the Connecticut state experience section). The law established a career ladder for early care and education providers and developed statewide accreditation sites to provide support toward NAEYC accreditation. A variety of strategies includes grants for professional development leading to the Child Development Associate (CDA) credential, for mentor training in accordance with the Head Start requirements, and for other training and higher education. Grants also may be used for developing a family child care network that will include provider training and support activities.

- *Oklahoma* legislators approved $1.3 million in new funds to establish statewide entry-level teacher training and provide college tuition and CDA credential scholarships.
- *Massachusetts* legislators allocated funds for child care training sponsored by agencies that provide child care resource and referral services.
- *Michigan* has increased funding for early care and education training and is targeting settings that provide services to low-income children by appropriating the funds specifically for the training of in-home and relative providers. Funds are set aside to provide financial incentives to providers who complete their training.[83]

Training Linked to Welfare Reform
Several states link child care training to welfare reform. One state strategy is to train welfare recipients for work in the early childhood field. Proponents of this strategy suggest that, with changes in welfare policies, more child care services are needed and that work as a child care provider is an opportunity for someone entering the workforce. Early childhood educators caution that adequate training and an interest in work with young children are prerequisites for successful training candidates. Another consideration is whether the trainee will be able to recruit enough children to make a living as a family child care provider.

- *California* will establish an early care and education professional development program for welfare recipients in the community college system.
- *Colorado* has appropriated $25,000 for each of 10 pilot sites to provide training and education to welfare recipients who want to become child care providers. Site approaches vary, with some including workplace literacy programs and college credits and others offering on-the-job training. For more details see the Colorado state experience section on p. 51.

The strategy of training welfare recipients as child care providers has been developed in several other states, including *Massachusetts, New Jersey and Pennsylvania.*[84]

Wages and Benefits for Providers

When early childhood providers leave their positions, children's learning is interrupted and children feel abandoned. This is a particular concern in the early childhood field because one-third of all child care teachers leave their centers each year.[85] Low pay and lack of benefits is a primary reason for this high turnover rate. Child care teaching staff earn an average of $6.89 per hour or $12,058 per year. Family child care providers earn an average of $9,528 per year and unregulated providers earn an average $5,132 per year. In addition, the National Child Care Staffing Study found that only 18 percent of centers offer fully paid health coverage to teaching staff.[86]

Linking Training and Education with Better Compensation
Recognizing this concern, several states are exploring policies to link the professional education and training of providers with higher wages or benefits. In October 1997, President Clinton proposed a $300 million federal effort to make this linkage.[87] One promising state approach to education for providers is the TEACH project initiated in *North Carolina* and now under way in several other states.

- In 1993, the *North Carolina* legislature appropriated funds for the previously privately funded TEACH (Teacher Education and Compensation Helps) project at $1 million per year.

In 1997, the legislature added nearly $500,000 to TEACH to increase its funding level to $1.42 million.[88] In the TEACH project eligible child care teachers and family child care providers receive scholarships to complete college courses in early childhood education. Upon completion of their educational goal, center staff receive additional compensation in the form of a raise or bonus from their employer. The increased compensation is provided through an agreement between the TEACH project and the teacher's employer. The employer makes a commitment to pay participating teachers the increased compensation at the start of the program. In return for the scholarship and the increased compensation, participants commit to working at their center for at least six months to a year after completing their course work. The program has simultaneously and successfully addressed several difficult infrastructure issues, such as professional development, compensation and teacher turnover.[89] It has been implemented in several additional states. Under a licensure agreement with the North Carolina Program at Day Care Services Inc. in Chapel Hill, North Carolina, the program is currently underway in *Colorado, Florida, Georgia, Illinois* and *New York.*[90]

- Several states use a strategy that does not directly compensate the caregiver in wages but provides a valuable cash benefit linked to professional development. In *Illinois, Pennsylvania* and *Minnesota,* lawmakers created programs to assume or forgive higher education loans for students enrolled in a child development program.
- In *West Virginia* a statewide Labor Department apprenticeship program provides two years of training to staff who work in centers, which results in the participant receiving a nationally recognized Child Care Development Specialist certificate that also can be transferred to a community college for further study. When they complete the training, participants are eligible to be promoted to center teachers and can earn higher wages.
- Although not linked to more provider training or education, *Rhode Island* legislators addressed the health care benefit issue. Under its Rite Care program, the state gives family child care providers who serve state-subsidized children access to health insurance for themselves and their families.[91]

Two other states recently have improved child care workers' wages. *Nebraska* required that in-home providers receive the minimum wage and *California* funded a cost of living adjustment for providers.[92]

Resource and Referral Services

All states provide funds to child care resource and referral services (R&Rs), either with federal or state funds or by using the federal dependent care tax credit. Twenty-one states spend state funds for child care resource and referral services.[93] The work of R&Rs varies from state to state, depending on organization and goals. R&Rs have improved child care services in many states through various strategies, including:

- Assisting providers with regulatory requirements to ensure safety;
- Training child care providers at all levels of professional development with programs ranging from basic instruction for entry level employees to more advanced courses offered in affiliation with community colleges; and
- Connecting providers to educational resources.

Some selected state actions include:

- *Illinois'* support for R&R services includes funds to assist child care providers to become accredited. The state will promote collaborations with Head Start and state-funded prekindergarten programs, with an emphasis on filling gaps in services, such as infant and toddler care, as well as nontraditional hour care. *Illinois* funds 17 R&Rs statewide.

- In the 1997 session, *Minnesota* legislators enacted a law to provide ongoing funding of R&Rs to provide parent information and consultation, recruitment, and technical assistance and training for new providers.
- A recent *California* law requires R&Rs to co-locate in welfare offices to quickly communicate child care information to welfare recipients. Five counties that offered this service found that parents make better choices when they have this information. The state Department of Education has requested $9 million from the state budget to fund this program statewide.
- *Washington* state has developed several R&R initiatives that promote health linkages and consumer education. The initiatives include a system for providers that tracks immunizations of children in their care, a Medicaid outreach program to inform parents about applying for services, administration of a grant program for families with special needs children, including provider recruitment and training, and a consumer education campaign to help parents make good choices.[94]
- In *Colorado,* R&R services administer the TEACH Colorado program that provides scholarships for child care teachers and bonuses when they complete their training.

Preschool and Head Start

To address the inability of the market to provide an adequate supply of good child care services, some states have funded preschool and Head Start programs, which can enhance young children's readiness to learn. The High/Scope Perry Preschool Project study found that good early education programs for low-income children lead to academic success, better job achievement and half as many arrests later in life. Good programs usually include parent involvement, health and social services, and a variety of learning experiences.[95] Many of these state preschool initiatives are aimed at children from low-income families.

More than 30 states have a preschool program, usually half-day, typically for 3- and 4-year-olds, funded at various levels and with a range of requirements. In addition, 13 states and the District of Columbia provide supplemental funding for Head Start, an early childhood education program for children aged 3 to 5 who are poor or who have disabilities.[96] Funded by the federal government at $3.98 billion in FY 1997, Head Start requires a match from local grantees. Programs must include comprehensive services, such as health care, social services and parent involvement.

Investing in Preschool or Head Start

Many positive child and family outcomes of Head Start have been documented, including school success, parent employment, better access to services, and improved abilities for children and parents to cope with violence.[97] The General Accounting Office and U.S. Head Start Bureau have estimated that about one-third of eligible children are enrolled in state preschool or Head Start programs.[98] The National Education Goals Panel found that only 45 percent of children ages 3 to 5 from low-income families were enrolled in preschool programs in 1995, compared to 71 percent of children from high-income families.[99] Although this is changing, many preschool and Head Start programs are designed to provide a part-day program, rather than the full-day program required by most working parents. Early education services help children to enter school ready to learn. Because of this, some state legislators want to expand the access of working families to preschool and Head Start programs.

States have taken various approaches to prekindergarten programs. Many allow preschool programs to operate in various settings, including public schools, child care centers and homes, and Head Start programs. As with Head Start, most states target poor children in their prekindergarten programs. A proposed federal child care rule allows states to draw a portion of federal child care funds by matching state preschool funds.

Head Start Collaboration

The U.S. Head Start Bureau has initiated collaborative efforts in all 50 states. The purpose of the state collaboration grants is to create a visible, collaborative presence at the state level that can assist in the development of significant, multi-agency and public-private partnerships. Head Start has funded a liaison for Head Start in every state. The collaborations are intended to:

- *Help build early childhood systems and enhance access to comprehensive services for all low-income children;*
- *Encourage widespread collaboration between Head Start and other appropriate programs, services and initiatives, augmenting Head Start's capacity to be a partner in state initiatives on behalf of children and their families; and*
- *Facilitate the involvement of Head Start in state policies, plans, processes, and decisions that affect the Head Start target population and other low-income families.[100]*

The initiative also helps forge operational partnerships between Head Start and state child care systems. Activities include:

- *Enhancing Head Start by extending services to a full day for working families;*
- *Giving child care staff access to additional resources to improve quality.*

Head Start has its own performance standards and also is covered by licensing in states that license part-day programs. However, preschool programs operated by the schools, including Head Start, usually are not covered by licensing. Some states apply standards set by the Department of Education; others have very few appropriate standards, or very little enforcement power. In *Massachusetts* the Department of Education and the Head Start partnership project are encouraging schools with preschool programs to become accredited. Several states, including *Massachusetts* and *Michigan*, require by statute that programs operated by schools for preschool children must meet standards established by the licensing agency for private programs.[101]

State preschool programs

States that establish their own preschool programs invest not only money, but also the time required to coordinate the involvement of schools, community organizations and child care providers. Instead of adding only Head Start funds, these states have the opportunity to maintain control of program performance and accountability and can support local flexibility. States that choose a school-based preschool approach also can support school-based decision making.

- *Georgia* earmarks approximately $200 million of state lottery funds to offer free preschool to all 4-year-olds. Unlike any other state program, any 4-year-old is eligible, regardless of family income. A recent evaluation found higher academic skills, better school attendance and parent satisfaction among participants.
- *Kentucky's* $38 million preschool program serves 4-year-olds from families below 130 percent of the federal poverty level (FPL) or preschool-age children with disabilities. The program, which serves about three-quarters of income-eligible children, requires minimum standards of quality. Minimum standards cover such areas as staff qualifications, developmentally appropriate practice, nutrition, social services, comprehensive health services and parental involvement. This program represents a strong collaboration between the state Department of Education and Head Start. Evaluation results have found positive outcomes for participants.
- *Washington's* Early Childhood Education and Assistance Program, funded at $28.3 million in FY 1997, provides comprehensive preschool to more than 7,000 poor 4-year-olds—a substantial majority of eligible children. Programs are funded in a variety of early care and

education settings, including child care and schools. Under revised standards due in 1998, programs must meet some Head Start performance standards and some NAEYC standards. Participating children have had higher scores in language, motor skills and conceptual abilities than children who did not receive these services.

- The *Connecticut* legislature appropriated $87 million in state funds for two years for school readiness grants in FY 1998. Providers of these programs can include education agencies, family resource centers, child care providers, and preschool and Head Start agencies. Interagency collaboration and comprehensive services are required. (For more information, see the Connecticut state experience section on pp. 52–53.)

- *Ohio* legislators appropriated $83.7 million for Head Start for fiscal year 1998—in addition to $17.4 million for a state preschool program—to reach the state's goal of providing comprehensive early care and education services to all eligible children whose families desire them.[102] (For more information, see the Ohio state experience section on pp. 65–67.)

Preschool and Child Care Coordination

An increasing number of states are coordinating their child care subsidy systems with their preschool programs to improve availability and quality. Legislatures initiated these policies in many cases. With the work requirements of the new welfare system, child care and preschool coordination can help states address the needs of working parents at all income levels. Because Head Start and prekindergarten programs are typically half-day, several states use child care money to extend the day for the welfare and working poor populations. Although this strategy requires more coordination and long-term planning with various stakeholders, it helps parents who must work all day and may lead to more efficient delivery of early childhood services. Because these programs operate during school days only, policy makers also may want to examine ways to keep them open during school vacations and holidays. By coordinating preschool or Head Start programs with child care subsidy systems, states are improving early childhood care and education services. Some states are encouraging accreditation for all the three subsystems.

- To address the needs of low-income workers, *Ohio* focused on models for collaboration between child care, Head Start and preschool. (See box in the Ohio state experience section on p. 66.) In the last biennium, legislators earmarked $6 million per year for full-day Head Start or preschool—$3 million from the Head Start budget and $3 million from the welfare to work budget under the previous AFDC/JOBS system. A recent legislative oversight report found that the collaborative efforts resulted in more families and children receiving services.

- A 1997 school readiness bill enacted in *Connecticut* requires that the state departments of education and social services collaborate to provide full-day, year-round child care and education programs for children ages 3 and 4 whose parents are working or are in training programs. The grants will be awarded to towns in priority school districts where 40 percent or more students are eligible for free or discounted lunches.

- *Colorado's* 1997 consolidated child care program allows 12 pilot counties to pool their child care and preschool funds for locally designed purposes, including full-day, full-year services for children from birth to age 6. Participating counties have no mandatory maximum spending amount and the program has no state fiscal impact. Pilot counties must consolidate state preschool funds and child care subsidies and may use federal funding available through Head Start grantees and other school district federal funds for preschool services. The legislation requires the pilot programs to place special emphasis on families that participate in welfare-related work activities.

- In its 1996 welfare reform law, *Florida* coordinated the child care system and preschool by requiring that 75 percent of prekindergarten enrollees be comprised of children of low-income working parents or those in the welfare reform program. Under the law, child care waiting lists are to be considered in calculating prekindergarten funding allocations. The law also requires schools, child care and preschool providers to identify children who are eligible for subsidized care and who need an extended day and extended year program. A single point of entry for all publicly supported early childhood programs and collaborative agreements also is required.[103]

State Administrative Collaborations

Some states also have developed administrative and legislative structures to coordinate these services. Until recently, most states separated child care from their funding of early learning programs. They usually fell under the jurisdiction of different departments and different legislative committees. In both the executive and legislative branches, one agency or committee may have jurisdiction over child care, another over preschool and another over welfare. To address this fragmentation, several states developed one agency or legislative committee to handle issues related to children and families. Although this approach could cause administrators or policy makers to become more protective of their authority and responsibilities, it could result in better coordination of disadvantaged families' access to important services. It also can facilitate the evaluation of programs and make it easier for legislatures to hold administrators accountable.

- To complement the state's recently created Department of Children, Families and Learning, the *Minnesota* legislature created a comparable committee—the Family and Early Childhood Education Committee—that includes a budget division to coordinate state funding of relevant programs.
- The *Tennessee* legislature established a Joint Select Committee on Children and Youth in the late 1980s, which has effectively directed major reforms in family support policies. Comprised of legislative leaders, the select committee recommends legislation to the General Assembly's standing committees and provides oversight to promote integrated policy and program development. The committee has led efforts to establish family resource centers, restructure children's services financing, develop a statewide plan to fund and implement early childhood education and enact a juvenile violence prevention package that included family support and early childhood elements.
- To coordinate its early education and care programs, *Hawaii* enacted Good Beginnings, which includes an interdepartmental council comprised of the directors of state agencies that serve families.[104]

Adding Comprehensive Services

State legislatures are increasingly incorporating early care and education services into a system that provides families with comprehensive, flexible and concrete assistance no matter what agencies administer what program. Comprehensive services are needed by families who require a variety of services. This assistance can include parent education, home visits, job placement, health and social services, housing and transportation. State legislators are recognizing that the complex and uncoordinated array of services that address specific symptoms, rather than the range of family needs, are part of the system failure. Family support programs vary in setting, format and emphasis. Some focus primarily on a single outcome, while others have broadly defined goals.

Family Support for the Entire Family

Most state family support programs include an early childhood component, but focus on the entire family. States have successfully used programs for young children as a central resource for parenting classes, literacy tutoring and other education services, job training or health referrals. These centers sometimes are called family resource centers and are usually based in either a public school or a community agency. Placing programs in schools can be an effective way to reach parents, particularly teen parents who are completing high school. Although they require coordination of funding and rules with multiple service providers, these family support efforts represent a comprehensive approach that has been shown to improve the quality of early childhood initiatives.

State programs to improve the quality and comprehensiveness of programs may include:

- Family support services, either in a one-stop agency or a through a linking agency like an R&R;
- Funding support to child care and early education through the community mental health system; and
- Coordination between preschool, child care and Head Start programs (See previous section).

Some states have initiated legislation that supports coordination of providers to offer a range of early care and education services along with family support and health services.

- The *Connecticut* legislature initiated a 1997 school readiness grant program that integrates early care and education funding and supports community school readiness councils to plan and implement comprehensive preschool services. These include health, nutrition and family literacy services, as well as parent involvement and education. (For a more complete description, see the *Connecticut* state experience section on pp. 52–53.)
- *Colorado's* 1997 consolidated child care grant program provides $12 million for comprehensive early care and education services to local communities. Pilot communities are required to offer educationally enriched programs, health screenings and follow-ups, parent education, voluntary home visits, sound nutritional services, special needs services, staff development and family support. (For a more complete description, see the *Colorado* state experience section on pp. 49–50.)
- Under *North Carolina's* Smart Start initiative, some counties provide comprehensive services. The legislation allows counties to use early childhood funds for health and social services, as well as for direct early care and education services. Local boards—that must include families, educators, nonprofit organizations, service providers and representatives of community groups—use flexible funds to design and operate programs. (For a more complete description, see the *North Carolina* state experience section on pp. 63–64.)
- The *Oklahoma* legislature used $1 million in TANF savings to establish full-day, full-year early childhood programs for infants and toddlers using the Early Head Start Performance Standards, including comprehensive health and parent involvement services.
- As part of its education reform act of 1990, *Kentucky* established a Family Resource and Youth Service Center program in schools in which 20 percent of the students are eligible for free lunch. Services to families include health services and referrals, parent training, child care and counseling. Studies have shown that the program not only has reduced dropout rates, but also has improved academic proficiency, parental participation, involvement of school officials, and connections with community agencies. The state also developed a literacy program, Parent and Child Education. *Kentucky* also created a preschool program that has been found to improve academic performance, familiarity with books and social skills.[105]
- *Minnesota* invests substantially in several initiatives that support parents, including:
  - The Early Childhood Family Education (ECFE) initiative ($29.7 million for fiscal years 1998 and 1999);
  - Head Start ($37.5 million for fiscal years 1998 and 1999);
  - Learning Readiness ($20.7 million for fiscal years 1998 and 1999); and
  - Way to Grow ($950,000 for fiscal years 1998 and 1999).

ECFE is designed to enhance parental competence through parent discussion groups, parent-child interaction activities, home visits, early health screenings and resources. A recent evaluation of low-income participants in ECFE found improvements in parents' understanding of child development, parent-child interaction and awareness of their child. A 1992 ECFE parent outcome study revealed higher levels of self-esteem and support than before and an improvement in children's social skills, self-confidence, and language and communication skills.[106] (For a more complete description, see the Minnesota state experience section on pp. 60–62.)

- Another family support program that offers voluntary home visits is *Hawaii's* Healthy Start program, which targets mothers of high-risk newborns. Other states have modeled programs after this initiative, which has shown significant success in reducing child abuse and neglect.
- In its 1996 welfare reform law, *Florida* required state support services for families in subsidized child care, including transportation, child development programs, child nutrition, parent training and family counseling activities.[107]

FUNDING LOW-INCOME CHILD CARE

This chapter focuses on key issues relating to state systems of funding child care services for low-income children. These issues have important implications for affordability, access and quality. State legislators have been at the forefront of many of these policy decisions, which involve levels of funding, sources and allocations. In the wake of major changes in the 1996 federal welfare law that gives states more flexibility, legislators, governors and state executive branch administrators throughout the country have established child care policies that affect services for families that are working toward self-sufficiency. Three fundamental policies discussed in this section are:

- Eligibility—Who is served.
- Copayment (Sliding fee scales)—What a parent contributes to the cost.
- Reimbursement rates and mechanisms—What and how the state pays providers.

Families affected by these decisions include welfare recipients, former welfare recipients in jobs, training or education, and other low-income or moderate-income working families. The federal and state work participation requirements resulting from the 1996 Personal Responsibility and Work Opportunity Reconciliation Act (PRWORA) and earlier state laws contribute to a critical legislative dilemma about serving these families—development of a system that incorporates both short- and long-term goals. First, states are responsible for providing care to families on welfare that enables them to meet work requirements and achieve self-sufficiency. Second, states are developing policies that provide child care assistance to working poor families that may need it to sustain work and stay off welfare. Decisions about funding a child care assistance system for low- or moderate-income families also have key effects on the quality of care, which have important implications for child outcomes. Federal law prohibits the use of federal funds for welfare benefits after a family has received welfare for two years and is not participating in a work activity, although states can use state funds for welfare benefits after two years. States are requiring welfare recipients to engage in work activities at different times, some within less than two years. See Table 1 for a chart of specific state work requirements. Some states exempt welfare recipients from these requirements if no child care is available or if the state does not pay for child care for these families.

Table 1. Work Participation Activities

State	Participation Trigger
Alabama*	When determined work ready, no later than 24 months
Alaska	Within 24 months or sooner as determined by department
Arizona	Within 60 days
Arkansas	Within 24 months
California	Specified in employment plan
Colorado	Within 24 months
Connecticut	Must be compliant with program requirement to continue receiving benefits after 21 months

Table 1. Work Participation Activities (continued)

State	Participation Trigger
Delaware	After 24 months
Florida	Immediately
Georgia	When determined work ready, no later than 24 months
Hawaii	Immediate
Idaho	Department to determine
Illinois	Determined in employment plan
Indiana	Immediately
Iowa	Determined in employment plan
Kansas	When determined work ready, no later than 24 months
Kentucky*	Specified in employment contract, within two years
Louisiana	Immediately
Maine	Determined in employment plan
Maryland	After 3 months
Massachusetts	Within 60 days
Michigan	Immediately
Minnesota	Within 6 months
Mississippi	When determined work ready, no later than 24 months
Missouri*	Within 24 months
Montana	According to federal law
Nebraska	Immediately
Nevada	When determined work ready, no later than 24 months
New Hampshire	Immediately
New Jersey	As determined by the commissioner, must be within 24 months
New Mexico	No work requirement
New York	As soon as practical, within 24 months
North Carolina	Immediately
North Dakota	Department may determine
Ohio	Immediately
Oklahoma	Department to determine, must be within 24 months
Oregon	Immediately
Pennsylvania	Immediately, and after 24 months of assistance
Rhode Island	Specified in employment plan, must be in first 24 months
South Carolina	After 60 days
South Dakota	Department to determine
Tennessee	Responsibility contract to specify; recipient must function above 9th grade level to participate
Texas	Immediately
Utah	Determined in employment plan, must participate after receiving assistance for 24 months and only if client has obtained a high school diploma or equivalent
Vermont	After 15 months for two-parent family; after 30 months for single-parent family
Virginia	Within 90 days
Washington	Immediately
West Virginia	Immediately
Wisconsin	Immediately
Wyoming	Immediately

*Taken from State Plan, no statutory provision.
Prepared by Dana Reichert, National Conference of State Legislatures, 1997.

Eligibility

The new federal welfare law eliminates separate child care funding categories that previously were based on a family's welfare status. Now the federal government awards states the Child Care and Development Block Grant (CCDBG), along with the authority to decide who can receive subsidized care. (For a detailed description of the federal funding structure, see the box on p. 33.) In examining the child care funding system, it is important that state legislators consider the tradeoffs between who is eligible for child care assistance, how much a parent pays in copayment fees and how much money the state will reimburse child care providers for serving eligible children.

When determining child care eligibility for low-income families in 1997, states took several different approaches that have implications for availability and affordability. Examples of policy approaches include assuring child care eligibility for low-income families, whether or not they are on cash assistance; and establishing priority among those who are eligible.

Child Care Funding for Families that Are Income-Eligible

Under the previous Aid to Families with Dependent Children (AFDC) system, child care for families on welfare was an entitlement, so states were required by federal law to provide such assistance. Under PRWORA, no family has a child care entitlement and states are taking new approaches to assure child care to groups of low- or moderate-income families, whether they receive Temporary Assistance to Needy Families (TANF) or not. Several states provide funds to pay for child care for all families relative to a designated percentage of either the federal poverty level (FPL)—currently $13,330 for a family of three—or the state median income (SMI). State policy makers who have adopted this strategy either targeted a population and set a funding level to serve it or decided how much funding was available and determined who could be served with those funds. States that funded all income-eligible families tended to increase their child care appropriations or direct other funds to child care. Families within the eligibility range in these states are assured of receiving child care services, during that fiscal year, rather than being placed on a waiting list.

To make this commitment, states face conflicting issues, such as setting levels of income eligibility, provider reimbursement and parent copayment. To stretch resources to reach more families, administrators in some states that extended the income eligibility ceiling also raised parent fees. (See the copayment section on pp. 37–41 and the Illinois state experience on pp. 57–58.) As fiscal or economic conditions change, a state may regularly reconsider specific funding and eligibility levels.

- *Illinois* provided sufficient funds in 1997 to serve families below 50 percent of SMI ($21,819 gross per year for a family of three, or about 165 percent of the FPL), allowing families that currently receive services to remain eligible through June 1998 or until their incomes reach 60 percent of SMI ($26, 230 gross per year for a family of three), whichever occurs first.
- *Wisconsin* raised its overall funds to assure child care services to working families with incomes below 165 percent of the FPL ($21,995 per year for a family of three). The state increased its child care resources largely by budgeting more than $80 million from its federal welfare allocations in FY 1998.
- *Vermont* provides child care subsidies to families with incomes below 80 percent of SMI ($28,642 per year for a family of four). Since 1995, the legislature has prohibited the state from denying services to eligible children on the fee scale program without first returning to the legislature with a budget adjustment request. This has resulted in no waiting lists for eligible families.
- *Colorado* enacted a statewide minimum child care eligibility level of 130 percent of FPL

($17,329 per year for a family of three) in 1997 and plans to use an additional $20 million in federal funds to cover these families. The law allocates block grants to counties and allows counties to negotiate changes with the state, including raising eligibility to 185 percent of FPL ($24,661 per year for a family of three).

*   *Rhode Island* established an entitlement that allows the state to provide child care to all families earning at or below 185 percent of the FPL ($24,661 per year for a family of three).[108]

Minnesota, Washington, North Carolina and *Oklahoma* are among other states that directed funds to provide child care to all families below a certain income level.[109] *Minnesota's* addition of $99.2 million in state child care funds for the next biennium will eliminate the current waiting list of more than 3500 families, but may be insufficient to prevent a future waiting list.[110] Similarly, the *North Carolina* legislature added enough funds to provide child care to all families earning less that 75 percent of SMI ($28,092 per year), but the state may experience future waiting lists.[111] *Washington* transferred $152 million in federal welfare funds for child care to serve all families earning below 175 percent of the FPL (approximately $23,338 per year).[112]

Sources of Funding

States that allocated sufficient funds to provide child care to families of a specified income level used various sources, such as:

*   State general revenue,
*   Federal child care funds,
*   Federal welfare (Temporary Assistance for Needy Families) funds.

The federal welfare law allows states to transfer up to 30 percent of their federal welfare allocation to child care. States can exceed this limit only if they use the funds, but do not transfer them, for child care. Unless states transfer the TANF funds, the five-year lifetime limit on TANF eligibility applies to families that receive child care with nontransferred TANF funds, even if the family receives only a child care subsidy and no other welfare benefits. States have decided to use, but not transfer, TANF funds for child care for other reasons. In *Florida*, for example, state administrators kept the funds in TANF because they wanted the flexibility for when they must obligate the money that TANF gives states.[113] Under the CCDBG, states must obligate child care funds within two years; under TANF, however, states have five years. If the funds are not expended after two years, CCDBG rules require that states return the funds to the federal government.

Because of a recent strong economy, most state welfare caseloads have declined, allowing some states to use TANF dollars for child care.[114] In addition, the work participation requirements are lower during the first few years, further easing the state burden. Recent data indicates, however, that states are having difficulty meeting the two-parent family work requirements in the first year.[115] Building child care capacity in this fiscal environment takes into account long-term demand, but could come at the expense of job-related or transportation expenses for TANF recipients. Moreover, if a state's economy worsens, the state may need to reallocate the funds to TANF and either reduce the child care funds or find another source of funding. The American Public Welfare Association (APWA) found that at least 16 states plan to use TANF funds for child care.[116]

Wisconsin budgeted $83 million of its TANF funds for its child care expansion in FY 1998. This funding strategy has coincided with a 54 percent reduction in the state's welfare caseload during the past four years. By using this strategy, *Wisconsin* will serve all families that earn less than 165 percent of the FPL ($21,995 per year) and will require less than 16 percent of any family's income for its copayment. State policy makers used $20 million in TANF funds for child care in January 1997 to reduce the maximum copayment from 46 percent to 16 percent of income.[117] Families will be able to continue receiving child care assistance up to 200 percent of the FPL. *Wisconsin's* welfare caseload reduction has made it possible to invest more in child care and other support services.

Funds for Child Care

The child care block grant is a fund comprised of three different funding streams with different matching requirements, effective dates and processes for federal appropriations. However, despite the multiple sources of funding, the allocation of funds, earmarks and criteria are the same for all funds inside the child care block grant. In addition, Title XX, the Social Services Block Grant that is used by many states as a funding source for child care, is reduced by 15 percent until FY 2002.

The Three Types of Funding Streams that are Pooled into the Block Grant

Federal Discretionary Funds: A total of $7 billion is authorized in discretionary funding from FY 1996 through FY 2002. The discretionary funding, formerly known as the Child Care Development Block Grant, is authorized at $1 billion for each fiscal year, subject to the Congressional appropriations process.

Federal Mandatory Funds: A total of $13.9 billion in mandatory funds is available from FY 1997 through FY 2002. Mandatory funds are capped and remain an entitlement to the states. Each state is guaranteed a base allocation of mandatory child care funds each year from a pool of $7.2 billion of the total mandatory funding stream. State allocations are based on one of three options, whichever is greater: 1) the annual average of federal IV-A child care grants to the state between FY 1992—FY 1994; 2) the federal IV-A child care grants to the state in FY 1994; or 3) the federal IV-A child care grants to the state in FY 1995.

Federal Mandatory Funds that Require a State Match: To be eligible for mandatory child care matching funds, a state must obligate its base allocation by the end of the fiscal year and meet maintenance of effort requirements (see below). Approximately $6.7 billion of the total mandatory funding stream is available in matching funds. States can match these federal funds at their FY 1995 Medicaid matching rate (FMAP). Each state will receive its matching funds at the beginning of the federal fiscal year based on its estimates of its need for matching funds and its population of children under 13 years of age. At the end of the fiscal year, the U.S. Department of Health and Human Services will perform an audit of state matching fund expenditures and states will have to repay misused or unused matching funds. All unused funds will be redistributed to qualifying states.

State Maintenance of Effort: To qualify for child care matching funds, states must maintain 100 percent of their IV-A child care expenditures for either FY 1994 or FY 1995, whichever is higher.

Single Criteria For Child Care Block Grant

Entitlement: There is no federal guarantee or individual entitlement to child care, nor is there a federal guarantee of transitional child care. However, many states have existing state statutes providing a child care guarantee to those on welfare who are required to work or for those who leave welfare for work. The absence of a federal guarantee does not necessarily eliminate the remaining state statute. Some states also have waivers that allowed them to guarantee up to two years of transitional child care.

Earmarks and Set-Asides: All federal child care funds (discretionary, mandatory and matching) are subject to the same earmarks and set-asides. A minimum of 1 percent of aggregate funding is set aside for tribes and the secretary can set aside up to 2 percent. Each state must then meet limited requirements for administrative costs and quality that are earmarked from all three funding streams. The law limits the funds available for administrative costs to 5 percent. Report language allows the secretary to define administrative costs and a range of activities including, but not limited to, licensing, inspection, establishment and maintenance of computerized child care information and resource and referral service that are not considered administrative costs. States must spend no less than 4 percent of all of their total funds on quality.

Transferability into the Child Care Block Grant: States may transfer up to 30 percent of their TANF block grant to the child care block grant.

Source: APWA, NCSL, NGA Welfare Reform Briefing, September 9-10, 1996.

Priority populations within eligibility

A number of states have prioritized populations for eligibility and some prioritize waiting lists so that families with incomes at the lower levels receive child care services first. This policy limits who is served, but allows the state to focus on the families that policy makers decide have the greatest need. This nonentitlement approach also allows flexibility should changes occur in state budget projections. Some states emphasize child care for families on welfare or those that had been on welfare but earned just enough to become ineligible. Although this policy may help a state avoid penalties for failing to meet work requirements, other low-income families that are excluded from eligibility often are placed on waiting lists and could end up on welfare if sufficient child care assistance is not available. Examples of priority populations for child care eligibility set by states include:

- Families on welfare or making the transition from welfare to work.
- Families with lower incomes (*Arizona, Nebraska, New Hampshire*).
- Younger parents and those finishing school (*Iowa*).
- Children with disabilities (*Massachusetts, Tennessee*).[118]

Exempting Welfare Families with Infants from Work Requirements

Under the federal welfare law, states have the option to exempt TANF families from work participation requirements if their child is under age 1. This option may be attractive to states for several reasons:

- Infant care usually is more expensive than care for older children;
- Good infant care has been found to be less available than care for older children;[119] and
- Many believe that infants benefit from being at home with a parent.

States that choose this option can ease the burden for low-income families to find jobs and child care. Yet because of the federal time limit, states have an incentive to help parents quickly gain as much training and experience as possible to assist them in moving toward self-sufficiency.

- At least 20 states and the *District of Columbia* plan to or will exempt families with a child younger than 12 months from work requirements.
- At the opposite end of the range, at least 10 states plan to require parents to work after their child is 12 weeks old or face sanctions in their welfare grants.[120]
- Two other states, *Nebraska* and *Montana*, plan to require families to work after the child is six months old and in one state, *Virginia*, the work requirement takes effect when the child reaches 18 months.[121] *Nebraska* requires part-time work when the child is 12 weeks old.[122]

State Flexibility on Sanctions for Welfare Families with a Child Under Age Six

States are prohibited from sanctioning nonworking welfare families with a child under age six if parents cannot locate child care that is reasonably close, affordable, suitable and appropriate. States can define these terms broadly, thereby further reducing the burden on child care supply, but these families still face a five-year lifetime limit on welfare benefits, so states continue to have an incentive to foster job creation and child care.

Federal and State Child Care Tax Credits

Twenty-five states and the District of Columbia have child care income tax provisions. (See table 2.) Through these provisions, states recognize the work-related expenses of families that need child care. In addition, families that have child care expenses can claim the federal child care tax credit against federal taxes owed. The credit claimed is equal to a percentage of their

---

Iowa's Priority Populations for Child Care

- *In July 1997, Iowa made the first priority for child care eligibility those who earn at or below 125 percent of FPL ($16,663 per year for a family of three) and who are employed 30 hours per week and targeted three other populations for child care services in descending order of priority:*

  - *Adolescent parents who are pursuing a diploma or GED;*
  - *Parents under age 21 in post-secondary education or vocational training; and*
  - *Parents with special needs children at 155 percent of FPL ($20,662 per year for a family of three).[123]*

With significant funding increases during the past two years, state officials anticipate no child care waiting list for these populations. Iowa was one of the first states to extend child care coverage to families that became ineligible because of increased earnings and to establish a family investment plan for welfare recipients. Through these changes, Iowa's system has produced in a 15 percent increase in the number of participants with earnings in its first two years; however, this number has leveled off during the last two years.[124]

---

employment-related expenditures for any form of child care. Limits are $2,400 for one child and $4,800 for two or more children. Families in lower income levels are less likely to be able to claim the credit because they may lack tax liability and may not be able to spend to the limit of the allowable expenses. Child advocates recommend ways to use tax provisions to benefit low-income families, including:

- Offer a credit instead of a deduction;
- Make the credit refundable;
- Use sliding fee scales that favor low-income families; and
- Place the credit on the short tax form.[125]

Table 2. State Income Tax Provisions for Child Care*
(1995 unless noted)

States (with personal income taxes)**	Type of child care provision	Description	Refundable
Alabama	none		
Alaska	credit	16% of federal credit	yes
Arizona	none		
Arkansas	credit	10% of federal credit; 20% if accredited center for 3- to 5-year-olds	no, except accredited preschool
California	none		
Colorado	credit	50% of federal credit <$25,000; 30% of federal credit for $25,000-$35,000; 10% of federal credit for $35,000-$50,000	yes
Connecticut	none		
Delaware	credit	50% of federal credit	no
District of Columbia	credit	32% of federal credit	no
Georgia	none		

Table 2. State Income Tax Provisions for Child Care* (continued)
(1995 unless noted)

States (with personal income taxes)**	Type of child care provision	Description	Refundable
Hawaii	credit	25% of eligible expenses for <$22,000, sliding in $2,000 income increments to 15% for incomes >$40,000	yes
Idaho	deduction	deduct expenses eligible for federal credit	no
Illinois	none		
Indiana	none		
Iowa	credit	75% of federal credit <$10,000 65% for $10,000-$20,000 55% for $20,000-$25,000 50% for $25,000-$35,000 40% for $35,000-$40,000	yes
Kansas	credit	25% of federal credit	no
Kentucky	credit	20% of federal credit	no
Louisiana	credit	10% of federal credit but not >$25	no
Maine	credit	25% of federal credit	no
Maryland	deduction	deduct eligible federal expenses	no
Massachusetts	deduction	deduct maximum of $2,400 or $4,800	no
Michigan	none		
Minnesota	credit	100% of federal credit <$16,050; sliding in $350 income increments to no credit for incomes over $29,700	yes
Mississippi	none		
Missouri	none		
Montana	none		
Nebraska	credit	25% of federal credit	no
New Jersey	none		
New Mexico	credit	40% of eligible expenses up to $8/day	yes
New York (1996)	credit	60% of calculated federal credit <$10,000 sliding in equal increments to 20% for incomes over $14,000	yes
North Carolina	credit	for incomes <$25,000: 13% of federal expenses for child < 7 years and 9% for child 7 or older $25,000-$40,000: 11.5% for < 7 and 8% for 7+ over $40,000: 10% for <7 and 7% for 7+	no

Table 2. State Income Tax Provisions for Child Care* (continued)
(1995 unless noted)

States (with personal income taxes)**	Type of child care provision	Description	Refundable
North Dakota	none		
Ohio	credit	35% of federal credit for <$20,000; 25% for $20,000-$40,000	no
Oklahoma	credit	20% of federal credit	no
Oregon	credit	30% of federal expenses for <$5,000 15% for $5,000-$10,000 8% for $10,000-$15,000 6% for $15,000-$25,000 5% for $25,000-$35,000 4% for $35,000-$45,000	no
Pennsylvania	none		
Rhode Island	credit	27.5% of federal credit	no
South Carolina	credit	7% of eligible federal expenses	no
Utah	none		
Vermont	credit	25% of federal credit	no
Virginia	deduction	deduct eligible federal expenses	no
West Virginia	none		
Wisconsin	none		

* This chart was compiled from two main sources augmented by telephone interviews. These sources are: Steinschneider, Campbell and Williams. 1994. *Making care less taxing: Improving state child and dependent care tax provisions.* Washington, D.C.: National Women's Law Center; and Gold and Liebschutz. 1996. *State tax relief for the poor.* Albany, N.Y.: Rockefeller Institute of Government, Center for the Study of the States.

**Nine states do not tax personal income: Alaska, Florida, Nevada, New Hampshire, South Dakota, Tennessee, Texas, Washington and Wyoming.

Source: Anne Mitchell, Louise Stoney and Harriet Dichter, *Financing Child Care in the United States: An Illustrative Catalog of Current Strategies,* Ewing Marion Kauffman Foundation and The Pew Charitable Trusts, 1997, 33-34.

Copayments (Sliding Fee Scales)

States are required to establish a parent fee structure and have flexibility to design it, including deciding which families pay how much of a copayment and the methods to determine the copayment. These policies have great implications for low-income families' ability to afford child care and achieve self-sufficiency.

Under the previous child care sliding fee scale system, states also had flexibility but were required to collect a copayment from families making a transition from welfare and were prohibited from requiring a fee from welfare recipients. Now, families that receive welfare no longer are exempt from a copayment so states are specifying this policy, including maintaining the copayment exemption or adding a copayment requirement. The new federal child care system has prompted states to reexamine key issues regarding their fee scales, such as deciding what percentage of income a low-income family should pay for child care. States typically establish copayments on a sliding fee scale so that those with the lowest incomes pay a smaller percentage of their incomes for child care.

In considering changes to their sliding fee scales, state legislators face policy questions and may have to balance several conflicting demands.

- *On what percentage of a family's income should copayments be based?* In deciding levels, legislators, governors and administrators in some states examine total available resources; some state decision makers examine what parent contribution is affordable, and some balance a family's ability to pay with available funding. Federal law requires states to allow families that receive a child care subsidy to have the same access to care as do unsubsidized families. The percentage of income that a family must spend on child care is an element of equal access.[126]
- *Should all families pay something or should some families be exempt from a copayment?* Policy makers who are examining this question balance affordability with a policy of shared responsibility for costs.
- *Should the copayment be connected with the cost of care that a parent chooses or be based solely on a family's income, size or numbers of children in care?* Because lower-cost care often means lower-quality care, legislators and other stakeholders have considered whether copayments based on cost of care promote worse care for low-income families.

Determining the method for a copayment
State policy makers typically choose from among four factors to decide the sliding fee structure:

1. Family income;
2. Welfare status;
3. Family size; and
4. Cost of care.

Income levels: Deciding who pays what fee for child care
A common state approach to deciding parent fees is developing an income-based scale. Although most options existed before the recent federal welfare law was enacted, states took several different approaches in 1997:

- Limiting copayments to a percentage of family income;
- Exempting certain poor families from a copayment; or
- Requiring fees from families that previously were exempt.

Copayment limits
Studies have documented the disproportionate share of child care expenses as a percentage of poor families' income. Although fewer than 40 percent of poor families pay for child care, those who do spend a significant portion of their budgets on child care.[127] To help guide state decision making on this issue, the U.S. Department of Health and Human Services suggested a maximum copayment limit of 10 percent of family income in its proposed child care rules, released in July 1997.[128] HHS has recommended use of this percentage since shortly after the federal welfare law was enacted in August 1996.[129] A number of state maximum copayment levels are approximately 10 percent, while other states limit fees at higher or lower percentages.

Poor families spent an average of 18 percent of their incomes on child care in 1993, compared to 7 percent for non-poor families, according to the U.S. Census Bureau. Families with the lowest incomes spent the highest proportion of their incomes on child care. Those earning less than $1,200 per month spent nearly one-fourth of their incomes on child care on average.[130] A child care economist and researcher projected that a single mother who earned the minimum wage ($8,840 per year) and had one child would have spent 38 percent of her income to purchase formal child care in 1995, creating a financial incentive to find lower-cost, informal care. This estimate was based on the average child care cost of $1.60 per hour, which totals $3,328 per child per year for full-time care.[131]

Copayment limits

Some states with copayments that are higher than the 10 percent proposed federal limit illustrate the tradeoffs between providing child care assistance to more families and increasing their fees.

- *The Illinois legislature increased the income eligibility limit of 50 percent of the SMI ($21,819 gross per year for a family of three) from the governor's proposed 40 percent of the SMI ($17,456 per year for a family of three), and added $100 million in additional state child care funds, instead of the $70 million proposed by the governor. The change in the law resulted in a higher percentage of parents' income used for the copayment. Even the highest income-eligible family of three, however, will pay no more than 13 percent of its income on child care.[132]*
- *In Wisconsin, policy makers initially required some families to pay about 46 percent of their incomes on child care within the established eligibility limit and with available funding. After considerable public concern, state administrators used federal TANF money to lower the copayment maximum to about 15 percent of a family's income. Although the state reduced its emphasis on cost of care, copayments still include a differential, so families that use less regulated (provisional) care are charged 30 percent less than families that choose licensed care. For example, a Wisconsin family of three earning 130 percent of the FPL (about $1,500 per month), with children in licensed care would pay about 13 percent of its income on child care—or $190 per month—compared to 9 percent of income—or about $130 per month—for provisional care.[133]*

What Is Affordable?

Economic analyses have not conclusively determined what percentage of income is affordable for low-income families to spend on child care, considering their other essential expenses such as taxes, shelter, food, health care, clothing and transportation. Researcher Teresa Vast of Hawaii, however, has estimated what families can afford to pay for child care by adapting the federal methodology used to determine what families can pay toward college costs.

Low-income families are expected to contribute approximately 22 percent of their discretionary income toward the expenses of a child attending college. Using this measure of affordability, Vast estimates that the percentage of gross income that a low-income family of three can pay for child care varies from zero to 8 percent.

Her analysis shows that poor families cannot afford to contribute to child care costs until their income reaches about 160 percent of FPL ($21,328 per year) based on the poverty guidelines for the 48 contiguous states (poverty guidelines for Alaska and Hawaii are higher). Families at this income level can be expected to pay just 1 percent of their income—$17 per month or $208 per year. At 200 percent of the FPL ($26,660 per year), a family could be expected to contribute 4 percent of its annual income for child care ($1,056 per year). Even at 300 percent of the FPL ($39,990 per year), families of three can pay just 8 percent of their income for child care ($3,346 per year or $279 per month), still shy of the cost of full-time quality child care in communities across the nation.[134] Table 3 shows Vast's estimates of affordability of child care for a family of three.

Table 3. One Estimate of Affordability of Child Care for a Family of Three

1997 Federal Poverty Guidelines for the 48 contiguous states	Gross Annual Income	Expected Family Contribution for Child Care Annual	Expected Family Contribution for Child Care Monthly	% Gross Income for Child Care (or college)	% Discretionary Income for Child Care (or college)
100%	$13,330	0	0	0	0
150%	$19,995	0	0	0	0
160%	$21,328	$208	$17	1%	22%
175%	$23,328	$526	$44	2%	22%
200%	$26,660	$1,056	$88	4%	22%
250%	$33,325	$2,117	$176	6%	22%
300%	$39,990	$3,346	$279	8%	23%

Note: The expected family contribution (EFC) for child care is estimated using a modified federal formula. See U.S. Department of Education, Student Financial Assistance Programs. *The EFC Formula Book: The Expected Family Contribution for Federal Financial Aid,* 1997-98. Additional information about the analysis used to estimate the EFC for child care is available from Teresa Vast, 701 Old Mokapu Road, Kailua, HI 96734.

The cliff effect and state examples of sliding fee scales
The limited copayment level has important effects on the highest income-eligible families' ability to afford child care and other expenses once their child care assistance ends. As a family's income increases to the point of ineligibility for child care assistance, state legislators may want to factor in the phase-out rate of other means-tested benefits and the availability and amounts of tax credits for poor families. The low-income family's loss of several public benefits—such as child care or Medicaid—when it reaches a certain income level is known as the cliff effect.

In deciding a sliding fee scale, state policy makers consider affordability issues for families earning at the high, low and middle points of the income scale. Figures 3, 4, 5 and 6 illustrate various state approaches to sliding fee scales.

Exemption Policies
Contributing to Affordability: Parent Fee Exemptions
At least 10 states plan to continue or add a copayment exemption for certain poor families.[135] These policies help make the cost of child care more affordable for poor families. As the parent contributes less, the state must provide more funding to serve the same families. Some states that exempted more families increased appropriations. Examples include:

• Exempting families on welfare from paying a fee (*New Hampshire, Mississippi*)
• Exempting certain other poor families from paying a fee (*California, Nebraska, Arkansas*)[136]

Requiring a Fee from Parents Who Formerly Were Exempt
To serve more families or otherwise increase their child care funding levels, some states raised parent fees or required more families to pay a fee. At least seven states plan to increase copayments for low-income families or add a copayment requirement for welfare recipients.[137] Policy makers in some states argued for higher fees because they thought the previous fee was too low and estimated that the higher fees would generate revenue. In some cases, however, it may cost more to administer a copayment for previously exempt families than the amount raised in revenue. Although some state decision makers argue that a copayment is a way for a parent to learn responsibility, this policy can increase the burden on poor families. Higher fee policies, however, helped states such as *Illinois* and *North Carolina* provide child care to more families.

Figure 3. California Fee Scale–Family of 3

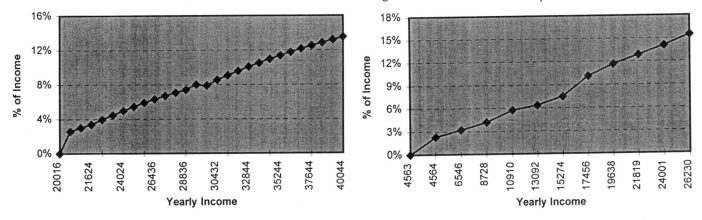

Figure 4. Illinois Fee Scale–Family of 3

Figure 5. Rhode Island Fee Scale–Family of 3

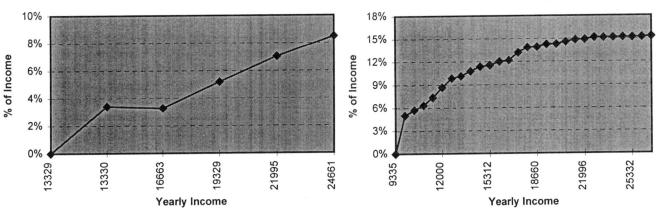

Figure 6. Wisconsin Fee Scale–Family of 3 in Licensed Care

Note: Based on FY 1998 state data. All families included in the scales in *Illinois, Wisconsin,* and *Rhode Island* are assured of receiving child care assistance in the next fiscal year.

Using family size in a fee scale: Factors to consider

Some states add to the parent fee if an additional child is in care. This policy may make care less affordable for eligible families, but charging little or nothing for a second child may conflict with other state policies aimed at discouraging families from having more children in subsidized care.

Using the Cost of Care to Determine the Copayment

In addition to a family's income and size, several states base copayments on the cost of child care. Under this policy, a family pays more for care that meets higher standards because that care is more expensive. This policy may discourage eligible families with limited resources from choosing higher-cost care, which often includes higher quality care. Policy makers who use this strategy may want to consider the long-term effects of placing low-income children in settings that may fail to positively contribute to their development or that may actually harm development. Because recent early childhood brain research suggests that the first three years are crucial to learning and development, cost-based fee scales have lasting implications. Two states—*Delaware* and *Louisiana*—used a cost-of-care scale and were able to maintain a maximum fee that is less than 10 percent of an eligible family's income.[138]

Reimbursement Rates and Mechanisms

Another major factor to consider when examining child care eligibility, funding and copayment policies is the level of reimbursement. Adequate reimbursement rates are critical to the effort to maintain a child care strategy that achieves both work force and child development goals. With adequate reimbursement, providers can pay for better services, such as more training, better wages or benefits. If rates are too low, fewer child care providers will accept subsidized children because providers—generally operating on tight budgets—are less able to afford to serve them. Reimbursement rates represent a tradeoff: On the one hand, states that raise reimbursement rates without increasing child care funding levels may face a reduction in the number of children served. On the other hand, significantly reducing reimbursement levels in an effort to spread resources further may adversely affect the safety and quality of child care and may limit access to care.

States consider a number of options when deciding what to reimburse child care providers, including:

- Paying at a percentage of market rates;
- Paying more to providers for better or harder-to-find care; and
- Paying providers directly for child care for welfare recipients.

States also set policies regarding how to pay for subsidized care, including:

- Establishing contracts with providers;
- Providing vouchers for child care;
- Paying cash to parents; and
- Disregarding child care expenses from a working welfare recipient's income, which increases the cash assistance grant.

Market-Rate Based Reimbursement: The 75th Percentile

To meet the welfare law's requirement that states ensure equal access for subsidized children and for unsubsidized children, a proposed federal rule suggests that states pay at least the 75th percentile of market rates for child care.[139] See the box on p. 43, "Establishing the 75th Percentile" for more about this issue.

A state's provider reimbursement rate level and policy has a substantial effect on the safety and quality of care that can be purchased for low-income families. Through former and currently proposed regulations, federal policy makers set the 75th percentile as a measurement of a state's ability to offer a wide enough range of providers to include sufficient choices of good care. Some states reimburse at this level, others below it. At least one state—*California*—pays above this level.[140] As states pay higher reimbursement, more providers with higher costs and better services are more likely to agree to serve state-subsidized children.

Low reimbursement rates are a disincentive for providers to serve low-income children, and can reduce the supply of subsidized care. Supply may dwindle in states that reduce their rates far below what the market will bear. In 1990, the Children's Defense Fund reported that 26 states indicated that providers were unwilling to serve children subsidized by welfare-related child care funds because of low reimbursement rates.[141] At least 20 states raised or plan to raise their reimbursement rates in FY 1998, although it appears that at least two states will be paying below the 75th percentile of market rates.[142] Moreover, observers point out that, while some states reimburse providers at the 75th percentile of market rates, they may base their rates on outdated market rate surveys. Another state option is to reimburse providers at the rate they actually charge parents.

Establishing the 75th Percentile

There has been much confusion about what the term 75th percentile means and how it is calculated. The 75th percentile is the rate at or below which at least 75 percent of the providers in a category charge.

To determine the 75th percentile, all the rates (or slots) in a category are ranked from lowest to highest. It is then necessary to count three-quarters of the way up the list to identify those rates that fall within the 75th percentile. The number separating the 75 percent of providers (or slots) with the lowest rates from the 25 percent with the highest rates is the 75th percentile.

Assume, for example, that there are four providers in a community. One of those providers has six toddler slots at $95 each; another has two toddler slots at $85 each; a third has three toddler slots at $75 each; and the fourth has one toddler slot at $70. In this case, the 75th percentile would be calculated as follows:

	By Slot:		By Provider:
	$95		$95
	95	75th Percentile	$85
	95		
75th Percentile	95		$75
	95		$70
	95		
	85		
	85		
	75		
	75		
	75		
	70		

Source: Louise Stoney, *Promoting Access to Quality Child Care: Critical Steps in Conducting Market Rate Surveys and Establishing Rate Policies,* Children's Defense Fund, October 1994, 44.

Differential Reimbursement
To encourage better quality or harder to find child care services, some state legislatures are increasing reimbursement rates to providers of those services—or differential reimbursement rates. Some states reimburse providers at a higher level to encourage care that is in short supply or higher quality care. States can pay a higher reimbursement rate to certain providers to encourage poor children's access to better or harder to find care. Although these differential rates will cost a state more, it also may lead to a greater supply of child care services that promote either stronger work force participation or better child development outcomes. The following are examples of such policies, including states that pay or are planning to pay differential reimbursement rates.

State Differential Reimbursement Policies
*   Accredited Child Care—Some states pay more for programs that receive national accreditation or that meet standards that promote healthy child development (*Connecticut, Mississippi, Oklahoma, Kentucky, Minnesota, New Jersey, South Carolina, Vermont* and *Wisconsin*).[143] Several more states have authorized higher rates for such programs (*Arizona, Colorado, Maine* and *Ohio*).[144]
*   More strictly regulated child care—Some states with multiple levels of regulatory requirements for centers or family child care providers require a higher reimbursement for providers that meet stricter licensing standards (*Florida, Iowa, Nebraska, New Mexico, North Carolina, Oklahoma* and *Wisconsin*).[145]

- Weekend, Early Morning, Evening or Night Care—Because there are few providers that can serve the increasing number of low-income families that are working at jobs outside the traditional hours of 9 to 5, a couple of states authorize a higher rate to providers that serve these families (*Colorado* and *Kentucky*).[146] A few other states (*Alaska, New Jersey, Louisiana,* and *Minnesota*) direct resources to providers that serve children during nontraditional hours.[147] An *Illinois* law requires the state to develop a plan to improve child care services during nontraditional hours. *Iowa* has proposed an additional 10 percent in reimbursement rates and *Ohio* expects a 3 percent increase in the rate for off-shift care.[148]
- Care for Children of Low-Income Families—With significant child care supply and affordability challenges for poor families, *Iowa* is proposing to pay more to providers that serve at least 50 percent to 75 percent state-subsidized children.[149]

Recent Selected State Reimbursement Rate Actions

- The *Rhode Island* legislature used part of its $6.8 million child care state funding increase in FY 1998 to increase provider reimbursement rates. The state's timetable includes a 14 percent increase in 1999 and a 9 percent increase in 2000 so that reimbursement rates reach the 75th percentile by 2000. The law requires that a new study be conducted in 1998 (and biennially thereafter) to ensure that rates are current. This will be the state's first rate increase since 1991.
- *California* reimburses providers at 1.5 standard deviations from the market rate, which is approximately the 93rd percentile of market rates.
- *Massachusetts* appropriated $25 million to raise reimbursement rates to between the 55th and 60th percentile of market rates (depending on type of care and region) in FY 1997.
- *Vermont* spent $1 million to increase reimbursement rates by 3 percent to the 75th percentile of market rates.
- *Colorado* administrators set reimbursement rate guidelines for counties based on a 1995 market rate survey, but the legislature in 1997 enacted a law to allow counties to set the rates.
- In 1995, the *Nebraska* legislature approved a minimum reimbursement rate at the 60th percentile of market rate after rates had dropped significantly.[150]

Payment Mechanisms

- **Contracts with providers**: One way states pay for child care is to negotiate contracts with providers. Because it guarantees child care slots, this method effectively establishes financial stability among providers in low-income areas, including urban or rural regions, or in cases of a short supply of child care for low-income families, such as nontraditional hour care. This mechanism also helps develop hard to find care. *California* legislators set aside about half the state's federal and state child care funds for direct contracts with centers in low-income areas. In return for a contract, state law requires these centers to meet higher standards than basic licensing.[152]
- **Vouchers**: States also provide vouchers or certificates to parents to purchase child care. This mechanism allows more flexibility in parental choice but offers less stability for low-income child care providers. To promote a range of provider payment options, as well as to maximize parental choice, a 1993 *Maine* law requires the state to provide both contracts and certificates for child care.[153]
- **Cash assistance to parents**: Some states reimburse parents with cash for their child care expenditures, either retroactively or with a cash advance. Child care providers often object to cash payments because there is no guarantee that the parent will use these funds to pay for child care. State administrators also have raised concerns about the lack of accountability when cash is used as the payment method for subsidized care.[154]

Reimbursing Family Child Care Providers for Meals

The new federal welfare law included cuts and other revisions in the Child and Adult Care Food Program (CACFP). Funding was cut by $2.3 billion over six years in CACFP, an entitlement program providing nutrition-related reimbursement to certain care providers, including child care providers serving low-income populations. Chief among these changes is the establishment of a means test for some family homes. Tier I providers continue to receive current reimbursement levels for meals served. These providers include those located within neighborhoods where at least 50 percent of families have incomes under 185 percent of the poverty level. Homes operated by a provider whose family income is below that level are also reimbursed at current rates. Tier II providers can opt to implement a means test for receipt of full reimbursement for children with low incomes and reduced rates for children from higher income families. They can choose not to establish a means test and receive significantly reduced rates for all meals served. The Tier II rates are reduced from 86 cents, $1.75, and 47 cents to 27 cents, 95 cents, and 13 cents for breakfast, lunch and snack, respectively. The legislation appropriates $5 million for one-time grants to states to help implement the means test. Other provisions include a reduction in the inflation adjustment for all family child care homes and elimination of reimbursement for an additional snack or meal served to children in centers for more than eight hours. States are no longer required to conduct outreach for the program. Child care experts caution that these changes may affect not only the supply of child care for low-income children, but also the quality of care. Participation in the program provided additional incentives for providers to obtain licensure, and CACFP personnel offered supplemental support and oversight of participating providers, many of whom may now simply find it easier to drop out of the program. At least one state, Vermont, has addressed this issue by appropriating $260,000 in its FY 1998 budget to replace the federal reduction in reimbursement to Tier II family child care providers.[151]

- **The disregard:** The federal welfare law allows states to continue to use the "child care disregard" as a retroactive, indirect child care payment mechanism to welfare parents under the TANF program. Under AFDC, states could reimburse parents indirectly for child care expenses by not counting some monthly income when calculating cash benefit levels. Many states used this option to increase the grants of welfare recipients who are in work and training programs after the recipients have paid for their child care. Instead of receiving a child care subsidy, a parent remains eligible for welfare payments for a longer period of time. When the former system allowed families to remain on AFDC without limit and entitled child care to such families, the disregard provided families with at least a minimal benefit. With the end of all federal child care entitlements and because TANF is limited to five years per recipient, this benefit of the disregard is gone.[155] This year approximately 10 states have eliminated or plan to eliminate the child care disregard, although some states continue its use.[156] As a result of eliminating the disregard several years ago, *Illinois* placed more welfare recipients into work and more of these families left cash assistance.[157]

STATE EXPERIENCES

State legislatures nationwide face many of the same issues in child care policy making, but each state responds to unique economic, political and social conditions as it designs early care and education policies. The following descriptions of state experiences illustrate the ways in which state lawmakers in nine states have developed child care policies over several years. These legislators have deliberated and created policies related to many of the issue areas presented in the preceding section. They provide examples of different approaches and their experiences may serve as examples to other states.

These states were selected because they are approaching child care policymaking in a variety of ways. By presenting experiences from these nine states, the authors by no means intend to diminish the innovations adopted by other states; space limitations prevent inclusion of additional information about other states' child care policymaking. The selected states have a combination of approaches that may apply to other states and that generally include:

- A policy agenda with a broad set of child care issues;
- Innovative financial strategies for low-income families;
- Approaches to improve provider training and development;
- Creative regulatory policies;
- Public and private partnership experiences; and
- Innovative efforts to develop state capacity to serve working families.

Each state experience begins with a list of the major issues addressed by that state's legislature. The list will guide your reading through a variety of approaches to each issue described in the other sections of the guide.

California

- Adding Resources to Low-income Child Care
- A Payment System that Promotes Good Care for Low-income Families
- Financial and Program Benefits of Contracts
- Affordability in the Sliding Fee Scale

Demographic Information

1995 Population: 31,589,153*
1995 Child Population (under 18): 9,176,000*
Children under 18 as percent of population: 29%*
1995 Children under 5: 2,809,826*
1995 Poverty Rate (all people): 16.7%*

Poor Children under 6, 1990-1992: 815,687**
Children under 6 Poverty Rate, 1990-1992: 25.6%

Number of Children under 18 with Working Parents(s): 4,349,699†
Percent of Children under 18 with Working Parent(s): 56%†

State Median Income: $48,755

Licensed Child Care Centers: 12,773

Licensed Family Child Care Providers: 52,199 (approximation)

Sources:
* 1995 Census Bureau tables
**Map and Track, National Center for Children in Poverty, Appendix C
†Working Mother "State of the States," May 1996
(4-person family, fiscal year 1997), Federal Register 61, 54: 11213
1997 Child Day Care Center Licensing Study, Children's Foundation
1997 Family Child Care Licensing Study, Children's Foundation

The California Legislature addressed key welfare-related child care in 1997 as the state experienced better budgetary conditions. First, welfare caseloads dropped for the first time in the 1990s, freeing state TANF funds. Second, unemployment eased, increasing state revenues.

Adding Resources to Low-Income Child Care

Because of the state's strong economic performance, the Legislature was able to add significant appropriations to the state's subsidized child care budget—including more than $60 million in state funds for child care for working poor families—and to direct more than $100 million of TANF funds to child care for welfare recipients.[158] Legislators expect that all TANF families that need child care—and those leaving TANF because of earnings—that are eligible for subsidized care will receive it. The new funds will serve a sizable percentage of working poor families that have been on waiting lists. In addition, the Legislature appropriated $25 million for a revolving loan fund that is used primarily for portable child care buildings. The state established a child care facilities loan fund with an additional $7 million for child care centers.[159]

A Payment System that Promotes Good Care for Low-income Families

With new research that emphasizes the importance of learning and development in the prekindergarten years and with studies that indicate that low-income families often have little access to quality child care, the California Legislature formulated a policy to address these issues. Lawmakers set aside about half the state's federal and state child care funds for direct contracts with centers that are located in low-income communities. As in most states, California has health and safety standards that all centers must meet to remain licensed. In return for a contract, state law requires those centers with contracts to meet higher standards than basic licensing, including:

- Better child-to-staff ratios;
- Stricter child development education and training requirements;
- Curriculum requirements;
- Support services for children and families; and
- Comprehensive state monitoring and review beyond the normal health and safety inspection.[160]

Financial and Program Benefits of Contracts

The state reimburses these centers at approximately the 75th percentile of market rates (about $105 per week for full-time care). Using this rate makes financial sense because the direct contract avoids the processing costs of vouchers or certificates, which are estimated to add 10 percent to 15 percent to California's cost of care.[161] These administrative savings translate into higher salaries for center teaching staff. Another benefit of the contract center is improved efficiency of state evaluations because an evaluator is likely to see more children for which the state pays a significant share of the costs. The result of this more efficient evaluation system is that evaluators can spend more time developing improvement plans with centers so that children are more ready to learn and have a stronger developmental experience.

Affordability in the Sliding Fee Scale
Although several states revised their child care fee schedule in 1997 to increase or add copayments to reduce a state's per-child spending and to stretch funding to provide a partial subsidy to more parents, California legislators decided against using a fee increase to fund expansion. The Legislature continued to exempt families below the poverty level from a fee, reasoning that the federal definition of poverty means that a family lacks enough money to purchase a full and nutritious diet and to meet other basic needs. Key legislators argued that requiring these families to make a child care copayment would constrict their food expenditures. Once a family's income exceeds the federal poverty level (FPL), parents pay a fee that increases with the family's income. The proportion of the family's income charged for child care also increases. A family of three earning just above the FPL pays about 2 percent of its gross income for child care. This fee increases to about 10 percent of gross income for families at 200 percent of the FPL, which is 75 percent of the state median income (SMI).[162]

State legislators rejected basing the fee on the cost of care because they reasoned that this policy would encourage parents to choose the cheapest care, which often is low quality. This is a long-term, two-generational attempt to break the cycle of poverty. Studies show that good early childhood development contributes to school success, which can help poor children achieve better jobs and economic self-sufficiency.

For more information, contact: Jack Hailey, California Senate Office of Research, (916) 445-1727.

Colorado

- Counties Decide Major Aspects of Child Care Financing
- Consolidated Child Care Pilot Programs
- Other Supply Strategies
- Training and Career Development
- Training Linked to Welfare Reform
- Licensing
- Innovative Funds for Training

The Colorado legislature delegated major child care subsidy decisions to counties in 1997 and, in addition, established pilot programs in 12 counties to coordinate early childhood programs to maximize resources and improve systems collaboration.

Counties Decide Major Aspects of Child Care Financing

Colorado committed to providing child care subsidies for low-income families, whether or not they receive cash assistance. State lawmakers enacted a statewide minimum child care eligibility level of 130 percent of FPL in 1997, and state administrators plan to use an additional $20 million in federal funds to serve all these families.[163]

Demographic Information

1995 Population: 3,746,585*
1995 Child Population (under 18): 1,015,000*
Children under 18 as percent of population: 27.1%*
1995 Children under 5: 268,950*
1995 Poverty Rate (all people): 8.8%*

Poor Children under 6, 1990-1992: 79,718**
Children under 6 Poverty Rate, 1990-1992: 24%**

Number of Children under 18 with Working Parent(s): 562,852†
Percent of Children under 18 with Working Parent(s): 65%†

State Median Income: $48,801

Licensed Child Care Centers: 2,291

Licensed Family Child Care Providers: 6,886

Sources:
* 1995 Census Bureau tables
** Map and Track, National Center for Children in Poverty, Appendix C
† Working Mother "State of the States," May 1996
(4-person family, fiscal year 1997), *Federal Register* 61, 54: 11213
1997 Child Day Care Center Licensing Study, Children's Foundation
1996 Family Child Care Licensing Study, Children's Foundation

Colorado law allocates child care block grants to counties and allows counties to negotiate changes with the state, including raising eligibility to 185 percent of FPL, changing state-set reimbursement rates or increasing reimbursement for scarce services such as weekend or night care. This policy of granting more local autonomy is consistent with Colorado's social services delivery system, which is administered by counties. Colorado administrators set reimbursement rate guidelines for counties based on a 1995 market rate survey, but the new law allows counties to establish a higher or lower rate than the one set by the state. Colorado also eliminated the use of the child care disregard this year.[164]

Colorado's devolution of child care financing authority in 1997 parallels other TANF policy decisions. Although welfare benefit and eligibility levels will be determined by the state, the welfare law gives counties block grants to determine the types of work activities for welfare recipients.[165]

Consolidated Child Care Pilot Programs

Colorado's consolidated child care program, enacted in 1997, allows 12 pilot counties to pool their child care and preschool funds for a range of purposes, including full-day, full-year services for children from birth to age 6. The law states that "Research demonstrates that there are positive outcomes for children in low-income families who receive quality child care services in their early, preschool years," and that consolidating funding "would allow for an integrated delivery system of quality programs for children in low-income families in Colorado's communities." Participating counties have no mandatory maximum spending amount. They must consolidate state preschool funds and child care subsidies and may use federal Head Start funds and other federal funds for preschool services. The legislation requires the pilot programs to emphasize families participating in welfare-related work activities and also provide educationally enriched programs, health screenings and follow-ups, parent education, voluntary home visits, sound nutritional services, special needs services, staff development and family support.[166] The enacting legislation has no fiscal note.

To assess the program's effectiveness, the law requires an evaluation by March 1999. It requires that the evaluation specifically examine:

- The feasibility of combining federal sources;
- The barriers to delivery of quality child care services; and
- Monitoring systems for overseeing the delivery of services under a system of community consolidated child care services.

Desired outcomes include:

- Consolidation or coordination of funding to create a seamless system;
- Collaboration among public and private stakeholders in the delivery of early childhood care and education; and
- Inclusion of the required components.

Other Supply Strategies
Recognizing the importance of good child care to the success of businesses, the governor's office established the Colorado Business Commission on Child Care Financing to recommend policies. The state has adopted several commission recommendations, including a program using bank-financed community development funds for loans to child care facilities to build or expand capacity. Another recommendation enacted by the legislature in 1996 was a dependent care income tax credit to assist low-income families with their child care costs. The state law provided a progressive rate credit with the following amounts:

- Families earning less than $25,000 per year receive a 50 percent tax credit for child care expenses;
- Families earning between $25,000 and $35,000 per year receive a 30 percent tax credit for child care expenses; and
- Families earning between $35,000 and $60,000 per year receive a 10 percent tax credit for child care expenses.[167]

Colorado also earmarked 20 percent of its crime prevention funds in 1996 for services to children under age 9. This initiative raised $2.2 million in 1997 and $1.4 million in 1996 for early childhood programs.[168]

Training and Career Development
Colorado has proposed a model early childhood professional credentialing system, including:

- Identifying core knowledge standards to allow for training across systems;
- Incorporating those standards into community college core early childhood courses and into the state's noncredit training;
- Including some of these standards in high schools and vocational programs for credit at community colleges;
- Coordinating training funds from the departments of human services and education for community-based learning clusters;
- Establishing a scholarship program that rewards providers with better compensation for completed additional training and education; and
- Encouraging the business community to invest in quality care.[169]

Training Linked to Welfare Reform

Colorado created another approach to increase child care supply in 1996 by training welfare recipients to provide early childhood services. The state appropriated funds for 10 pilot sites that will experiment with a variety of approaches to training and curriculum. These sites will receive grants of up to $25,000. The program requires grantees to describe their training program's design, purpose and type; recruitment strategies; and efforts to ensure support for successful participants to seek independent child care employment as well as support for their child care needs. The law also requires that grantees use community resources in developing their training programs.[170]

Licensing

Colorado has adopted a child care licensing policy that directs regulatory resources to centers that have a poor record or that need technical assistance or monitoring to consistently meet state regulatory minimum standards for health, safety, and practice.[171] This regulatory approach allows states to focus resources on centers where there are concerns for children's health and safety, while centers with good records are less frequently monitored.

Innovative Funds for Training

To establish better services, Colorado enacted a voluntary income tax check off for child care in 1996 to establish a child care improvement fund. The state provides these funds to programs that propose to improve child care quality standards, especially staff qualifications, training and development, staff-child interaction, family and staff partnerships and curriculum. Funds also can be used in the area of accreditation. Funds from this source enable the state to distribute nearly $119,000 to providers. Individual grants are limited to $1,000 each in order to distribute the funds to as many providers as possible.[172]

For more information, contact: Oxana Golden, Colorado Division of Child Care, (303) 866-5943.

Demographic Information

1995 Population: 3,274,662*
1995 Child Population (under 18): 869,000*
Children under 18 as percent of population: 26.5%*
1995 Children under 5: 227,592*
1995 Poverty Rate (all people): 9.7%*

Poor Children under 6, 1990-1992: 65,064**
Children under 6 Poverty Rate, 1990-1992: 20.1%**

Number of Children under 18 with Working Parent(s): 475,869†
Percent of Children under 18 with Working Parent(s): 64%†

State Median Income: $62,107

Licensed Child Care Centers: 1,640

Licensed Family Child Care Providers: 4,927

Sources:
* 1995 Census Bureau tables
** Map and Track, National Center for Children in Poverty, Appendix C
† Working Mother "State of the States," May 1996
(4-person family, fiscal year 1997), Federal Register 61, 54: 11213
1997 Child Day Care Center Licensing Study, Children's Foundation
Information provided by state, August 1996

Connecticut

- Early Care and Education Collaborations for Working Families
- Quality Enhancement Grants
- Using Reimbursement Rates to Encourage Better and Hard to Find Services
- Facilities Financing: A Creative Public-Private Partnership

In 1997 the Connecticut legislature created a school readiness prekindergarten grant program to address the needs of working families with preschool-age children. With $87 million in state funds appropriated for two years of a five-year phase-in, this law furthers child care and preschool coordination, mandates comprehensive services and creates innovative financing mechanisms.[173] Speaker of the House Thomas D. Ritter, who helped lead the initiative, said "For every dollar you spend in childhood intervention, you save $7 later on. If you have early child education, you are less likely to be in jail or on welfare or in special education. It's cost effective. If you start school without early childhood education, you are behind and you never catch up."[174]

Early Care and Education Collaborations for Working Families

Connecticut's law requires that the state departments of education and social services collaborate to provide grants to full-day, year-round child care and education programs for children ages 3 to 5 whose parents are working or are in training or education programs. The grants will be awarded to 14 cities designated as priority school districts, as well as to 14 municipalities that have schools where 40 percent or more of the students are eligible for free or discounted lunches. The legislation requires comprehensive services, including parent education, health referrals, nutrition services, family literacy referrals, racially and ethnically diverse admission policies, a transition plan to kindergarten, staff development and an annual evaluation.[175]

Eligible program providers include local and regional boards of education, regional educational service centers, family resource centers, child care providers, Head Start providers, preschool programs and other programs that meet state-set education standards. The agencies must provide a range of programs to meet the needs of all children, coordinate the services of school districts with private organizations and offer parental choice. This coordinated program builds on other recent efforts in Connecticut. The legislature appropriated state Head Start funds in 1995 for welfare-to-work participants in cities and towns that had a minimum number of welfare families. In 1996 legislators authorized the use of child care subsidies in coordination with Head Start programs.[176]

The legislature specified that the law's intent is to:

- Provide access for children to programs that promote health and safety;
- Prepare children for formal schooling;
- Encourage coordination among programs and prevent duplication of services;

- Provide local program flexibility;
- Prevent or minimize developmental delay among young children;
- Strengthen the family through parental involvement in a child's development and education; and
- Improve the availability and quality of school readiness programs.

Quality Enhancement Grants

The law incorporates research on good child care services by creating supplemental quality enhancement grants to help school readiness or child care providers obtain national accreditation, child development scholarships and training for mentor teachers under federal Head Start regulations. It requires that grants provide health services, parent education and community outreach programs. To accompany the quality enhancement grants, the law requires five regional accreditation projects with a priority for programs where at least a quarter of the children served live with families that earn less than 75 percent of the SMI.

Using Reimbursement Rates to Encourage Better and Hard to Find Services

As another incentive for higher quality or accredited early childhood programs, the law also authorizes the state to pay higher reimbursement rates to providers of such services. The new law encourages stronger licensing standards by requiring that the state establish a reimbursement system to account for differences in the type and cost of care provided by licensed and unlicensed caregivers and for program accreditation. The law also requires supplemental state reimbursement for programs that offer extended nontraditional hours and for those that serve children with special needs. State lawmakers established this provision to increase the currently limited supply of these programs. The law allows the executive branch to determine the amount of the reimbursement differentials.

The differential reimbursement rate policy for licensed providers continues the state's policy of providing incentives for child care licensing. In 1996 Connecticut enacted a law that promotes licensing by offering amnesty to unregulated family home or center providers that become licensed. The normal penalty for illegally unregulated child care providers is $100 per day.[177]

Facilities Financing: A Creative Public-Private Partnership

The law also enlists the help of Connecticut banks and a quasi-public agency within the state's Health and Education Facilities Authority to provide low-interest loans for construction or renovation of early childhood programs or for helping them comply with regulatory requirements. Modeled after an Illinois program, this initiative will market bonds to private investors. A portion of the debt service would be paid by the state Department of Social Services. The law also establishes a loan guarantee program for development or expansion of child care or development centers. Connecticut banks have agreed to establish a child care loan fund with an initial lending capacity of $10 million to $20 million. The state then would guarantee between 20 percent and 50 percent of the principal on these loans.[178]

To provide an incentive for good care, priorities for loan guarantees are to be given to financing facilities that obtain accreditation from the National Association for the Education of Young Children. The loan guarantee provision also promotes further coordination of services by requiring a priority for programs that are colocated with other services and those that are included in a school readiness plan. State legislative staff estimate that these funds over the next four years could provide from 2,100 to 6,300 new child care spaces requiring $30 million to $90 million in financing.[179]

For more information, contact: Elaine Zimmerman, Connecticut Commission on Children, (860) 240-0290.

Demographic Information

1995 Population: 14,165,570*
1995 Child Population (under 18): 3,512,000*
Children under 18 as percent of population: 24.8%*
1995 Children under 5: 967,861*
1995 Poverty Rate (all people): 16.2%*

Poor Children under 6, 1990-1992: 311,160**
Children under 6 Poverty Rate, 1990-1992: 27.4%**

Number of Children under 18 with Working Parent(s): 1,813,633†
Percent of Children under 18 with Working Parent(s): 63%†

State Median Income: $43,374

Licensed Child Care Centers: 5,686

Licensed Family Child Care Providers: 4,002

Sources:
* 1995 Census Bureau tables
** Map and Track, National Center for Children in Poverty, Appendix C
† Working Mother "State of the States," May 1996
(4 person family, fiscal year 1997), Federal Register 61, 54: 11213
Based on state reports, July 6, 1996

Florida

- Reducing the Waiting List and Serving Additional Families
- Florida's Child Care Partnership Act
- Coordinating Child Care with Preschool Programs
- Developing Good Care
- Developing Good Family Child Care
- More Initiatives to Improve Care

Over the years, Florida legislators have invested in several initiatives to expand access, affordability and quality of early childhood programs. Beginning with efforts in the 1980s to enlist business support for child care and to provide child care to teenage parents in public school, state policies exemplify a long-term vision. In the 1990s, Florida lawmakers led early childhood improvements in several areas, including innovative financing, public and private partnerships, systems coordination and quality enhancements. Evaluation research has guided the process.

Reducing the Waiting List and Serving Additional Families

To provide services to the more than 30,000 eligible children of the working poor on the child care waiting list, state lawmakers approved a $23 million increase in state child care funds for FY 1998. This amount, combined with federal child care and welfare funds, will enable the state to serve one-fourth of those on the waiting list. In 1997, Florida policy makers decided to use $89 million of the state's TANF funds for child care, but not to transfer it to the Child Care and Development Block Grant (CCDBG). State officials left this money in TANF because of greater flexibility; CCDBG rules require the state to obligate child care funds within two years, whereas TANF rules give states five years to decide how to spend the funds.[180]

Another Florida strategy to reduce the waiting list is to allow counties to develop children's services taxing districts that raise child care money. Six districts raised $63 million through this process in FY 1994-95, of which approximately $11 million is used for child care. This funding is used to both reduce the waiting list and improve services.[181]

Florida's eligibility groups are prioritized so that certain groups receive child care before others. In order of priority are abused and neglected children, welfare recipients, working poor and migrant families with incomes below the FPL, and working poor families between 100 percent and 150 percent of FPL. The vast majority of the state's waiting list is comprised of non-TANF working poor, since welfare families are served almost immediately.[182]

Florida's Child Care Partnership Act

The waiting list issue prompted legislators to consider how to involve employers in the solution. A federally-funded research project examined the employment patterns of families that used publicly-funded child care and the specific industries in which these families were employed. In widely publicized findings throughout the state and nationwide, the study identified specific industries that employed high numbers of workers who use subsidized child care. These industries included fast food, grocery chains, insurance, banking, restaurants, hotels, temporary services, health care and public administration.

The study results were an important factor that contributed to the legislative development of a system to secure business resources for low-income child care.[183] The state's 1996 welfare reform law established a public and private partnership to fund child care subsidies for low-income working families. The Legislature appropriated $2 million, to be matched by $2 million from businesses. Employers met the match and the Legislature doubled the state's share to $4 million in 1997.[184] Thirty Florida companies currently are contributing to the fund. Contributors include several retail businesses, such as fast food companies, health services and banks. Working families with incomes at or below 150 percent of the FPL qualify for the subsidy. The program is administered by the state's community coordinated child care agencies and child care resource and referral (CCR&R) programs.[185]

Coordinating Child Care with Preschool Programs

To maximize state resources for poor children, Florida's 1996 welfare reform law required that 75 percent of prekindergarten enrollees be comprised of children of low-income working parents or those in the welfare reform program. Child care waiting lists are to be considered in calculating prekindergarten funding allocations. The law requires schools and child care and preschool providers to identify children eligible for subsidized care who need an extended day and extended year program. It also mandates a single point of entry for all publicly-supported early childhood programs and collaborative agreements.[186]

Developing Good Care

Two 1991 Florida legislative measures improved child care quality. One law increased training requirements from 20 hours to 30 hours for all child care personnel. This law also required that every child care facility have at least one staff person with a child development associate (CDA) credential or equivalent for every 20 children. The other set child-to-staff ratios at a higher standard for children from birth to 5 years of age in early care and education programs.[187] A Families and Work Institute study of these policies found that:

- Children's intellectual and emotional development were improved;
- Teachers were more sensitive and responsive;
- Teachers' negative management styles (yelling, sarcasm, scolding) declined, sometimes by as much as 75 percent; and
- Global measures of the quality of the learning environment increased.[188]

To further encourage quality, the Legislature in 1996 initiated the "Gold Seal" program, which provides official recognition to centers that have been voluntarily accredited by the National Association for the Education of Young Children, the National Early Childhood Program Accreditation Commission, the National Association of Family Child Care and other nationally recognized accrediting associations whose standards meet or exceed those three.[189]

Developing Good Family Child Care

The state also funds a program to train and support family child care providers. Operated by the Florida Children's Forum, the program creates networks of family child care providers to expand the availability of infant care in family child care homes and to provide training and support.[190] A 1996 Florida law also encourages the growth of good family child care homes by charging regulated family child care homes residential utility rates and exempting them from the utility tax.[191]

More Initiatives to Improve Care

State policy makers have adopted other measures to improve child care. Florida requires the state to pay regulated child care providers at the prevailing market rate and unregulated providers at 50 percent of the market rate. The state also takes part in the TEACH (Teacher Education And Compensation Helps) program initiated in North Carolina. This program increases wages and benefits of providers that receive additional progressive training and education that lead to degrees in early childhood education. Another way the state has improved services for young children is by requiring comprehensive family support services. The 1996 welfare law required state support services for families in subsidized child care, including transportation, child development programs, child nutrition, parent training and family counseling activities.[192]

For more information, contact: Ron Cox, Florida Department of Children and Families, (904) 488-4900.

Illinois
- Funding Child Care for Poor Families
- Copayments
- Legislative Oversight of the Sliding Fee Scale
- Good Results from Better Reimbursement
- Encouraging More Good Care: Facility Financing
- Incentives for Better Providers

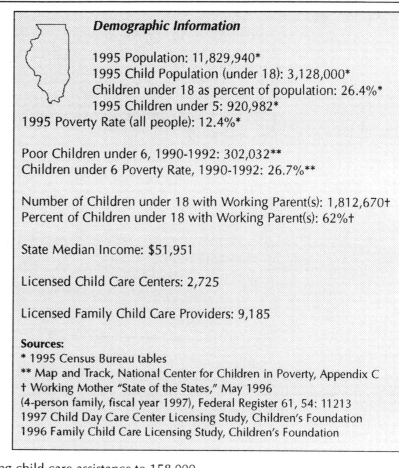

Demographic Information

1995 Population: 11,829,940*
1995 Child Population (under 18): 3,128,000*
Children under 18 as percent of population: 26.4%*
1995 Children under 5: 920,982*
1995 Poverty Rate (all people): 12.4%*

Poor Children under 6, 1990-1992: 302,032**
Children under 6 Poverty Rate, 1990-1992: 26.7%**

Number of Children under 18 with Working Parent(s): 1,812,670†
Percent of Children under 18 with Working Parent(s): 62%†

State Median Income: $51,951

Licensed Child Care Centers: 2,725

Licensed Family Child Care Providers: 9,185

Sources:
* 1995 Census Bureau tables
** Map and Track, National Center for Children in Poverty, Appendix C
† Working Mother "State of the States," May 1996
(4-person family, fiscal year 1997), Federal Register 61, 54: 11213
1997 Child Day Care Center Licensing Study, Children's Foundation
1996 Family Child Care Licensing Study, Children's Foundation

In a landmark policy decision, the Illinois legislature in 1997 appropriated funds that guarantee child care services to a defined population of the state's poor families, whether or not they are on welfare. Under the new system, all low-income families earning below 50 percent of SMI ($21,819 gross per year for a family of three, or about 165 percent of the FPL) will receive child care assistance. Families currently served are eligible through June 1998 or until their incomes reach 60 percent of SMI ($26,230 gross per year for a family of three), whichever occurs first.[193] The $100 million increase was approved with bipartisan support.[194] The new funds will allow the state to provide care to 59,000 additional children, bringing the total number of children receiving child care assistance to 158,000.

Under the previous system, families below 60 percent of SMI were eligible for child care, but only some families actually received services unless they were on welfare, in which case they were guaranteed child care assistance. In fact, the state required that providers give priority to families below 50 percent of SMI. Under the new system, nearly 60,000 more families will receive subsidized care, and state administrators expect that only a handful of families who received services before will not be served.[195]

Funding Child Care for Poor Families
The state child care funding increase for FY 1998 brings the total Illinois child care funding base to more than $223 million, in addition to its federal child care funds that total approximately $157 million. Recognizing that the new funding will largely eliminate Illinois' child care waiting list of nearly 30,000 children, a *Chicago Tribune* article stated, "The state's lawmakers deserve credit for recognizing the critical importance of child care to the economic future of those families and for allocating the money to help make that care available. The legislature has laid the groundwork for a better future for tens of thousands of families by recognizing unequivocally the pivotal role child care plays in their lives. That's a bold move—and a promising one."[196]

Copayments
Illinois policy makers and administrators faced a major policy tradeoff during this decision making process: increasing parent fees to serve more families. The governor proposed that the state add $70 million in state funds to set an eligibility limit at 40 percent of the SMI ($17,456 per year for a family of three). Under this proposal state administrators were prepared to set

a fee scale that limited copayments at about 10 percent of income for all eligible families. The legislature added $30 million to the governor's request and specified that the state serve child care to families up to 50 percent of the SMI. To serve these additional families with the appropriated funds, the state increased its maximum fee to about 13 percent of family income for a family of three, or $54 per week.[197] This scale is an increase from the state's previous system, which required only a 25 cent per week parent fee. The state tentatively estimates that, based on expected usage and patterns, the new scale will add more than $80 million to state revenues.[198]

The following example illustrates the tradeoffs between serving more families and increasing fees in Illinois. Under the new system, a mother with two children who earns $19,638 gross per year, or 45 percent of the SMI, is required to spend $44 per week, or 11.6 percent of her income on child care. With the 10 percent copayment, proposed by the federal government, this mother would pay about $38 per week. The difference is significant: approximately $310 per year or about $25 per month. If the legislature supported the governor's original proposal, which would have guaranteed eligibility up to 40 percent of the SMI, this mother would have received no subsidy. Even if she were able to find child care at $10 per day, her weekly cost would be about $50. Compared to the new fee schedule, she would pay more for child care that is possibly poorer quality.

Legislative Oversight of the Sliding Fee Scale
In October 1997, the legislature began review of the parent fee structure through the Joint Committee on Administrative Rules (JCAR), a bipartisan committee of 12 legislators from both the House and Senate. This joint committee reviews administrative rules established by the state agencies and can object to proposed rules, particularly if members believe the rules do not fulfill the law's intent. The agency can refuse to make changes recommended by the committee. State Senator Miguel del Valle requested postponement of the new fee scale until its effect could be assessed. He said, "Their goal to service more people is a valid one, but I don't think we should be doing that by raising the revenue from low-income families." Randy Valenti, the associate director of the state Office of Children and Families disagreed, saying, "The old fees were completely unrealistic. The service was very underpriced."[199] After a public comment period, state administrators made minor revisions in the sliding fee scale and, with the changes, JCAR took no action to further modify the scale.[200]

Building on a Successful "Work Pays" Policy
Illinois administrators will implement the new system in the context of its welfare-to-work program, Work Pays. Under Work Pays, initiated in 1993, welfare parents' grant levels are reduced at a slower rate relative to their earnings than under the previous policy ($1 reduction for every $3 of earnings). This provides recipients with more resources while they are on welfare and they remain eligible for welfare at higher incomes than before. With significant state funding increases to implement the policy, the number of working welfare families doubled in two years.[201]

Good Results from Better Reimbursement
By paying providers directly and eliminating the child care earned income disregard, as Illinois did a few years ago, the state has more working welfare recipients and fewer families that require cash assistance.[202] Now, reimbursement more closely reflects true child care costs than under the disregard and working welfare recipients no longer pay up front. The legislature has approved steady reimbursement rate increases in recent years and, although another increase failed in 1997, the new child care law requires a market rate study by July 1998.[203]

Encouraging More Good Care: Facility Financing
To sustain child care supply, the state has supported an innovative financing approach. By making capital available to child care centers, the Illinois Facilities Fund (IFF) has financed more

than $15 million in facilities funding during the past 10 years, creating spaces for 1,700 children in approximately 30 centers. In partnership with the state Department of Children and Family Services (DCFS), the IFF borrowed funds through the sale of tax-exempt bonds to develop centers in low-income communities. DCFS repaid the debt through 1997, when the program was transferred to the state Department of Human Services. The state will repay the loan over 12 years using state general funds.[204]

Incentives for Better Providers
To encourage more skilled child care providers, Illinois assumes or forgives loans for students in a child development program. The state has also developed the TEACH program, which pays more to those child care providers who seek progressive education to earn a degree. The new Illinois child care law also funds 17 child care resource and referral (R&R) programs throughout the state to help parents find quality care. R&R contracts will provide training, technical assistance and support for programs that are seeking accreditation.[205] These efforts will promote collaboration with Head Start and state-funded prekindergarten programs, and will focus on filling service gaps such as infant and toddler care and nontraditional hour care.

For more information, contact: Michele Piel, Illinois Department of Human Services, Child Care and Development, (312) 793-3610.

Minnesota

- Eliminating the Waiting List
- Prioritization of Child Care Waiting Lists
- Reimbursement Incentives and Policies
- Parent Involvement and Family Support
- Empowering Resource and Referrals to Help Providers and Parents
- Integrating Early Childhood Services into a Variety of Policies

In an unprecedented increase, the Minnesota Legislature appropriated enough low-income child care funding for the FY 1998-99 biennium to eliminate the state's current waiting list, which is comprised of low-income working families.

Eliminating the Waiting List

During the 1997 session, the Legislature and the governor focused on providing an increase in funding that was sufficient to eliminate the waiting list, which at the beginning of the session included 5,639 families. To provide child care to both TANF recipients and non-TANF low-income working families in the FY 1998-99 biennium, the state added $113.3 million, a 130 percent increase over the past biennium.[206] This includes an additional $4 million appropriated for child care development activities. The new funds will increase the number of welfare families served by 143 percent from FY 1997 to FY 1999 (7,874 in FY 1997 to 19,150 in FY 1999) and will increase the number of non-welfare, low-income families served by 37 percent during that time (10,192 in FY 1997 to 14,000 in FY 1999), according to state projections. In FY 1998 alone, the projected increases are 48.5 percent for welfare families and 28.5 percent for nonwelfare families. Although these increases will eliminate the state's current child care waiting list, the state expects that new cases will accumulate to a new waiting list.[207] Minnesota has given priority to families on the child care waiting list who are making the transition from welfare to work. Low-income working families who have never been on welfare are lower on the priority list.

Prioritization of Child Care Waiting Lists

The state's child care waiting list for the child care basic sliding fee scale is prioritized as follows.

1. Students in high school who are completing their general equivalency diploma, English as a second language or remedial training.
2. Working families that have received one year of child care assistance since becoming ineligible for welfare.
3. Families that have moved from a county where they were receiving child care to a county with 1st and 2nd priorities on the waiting list.
4. Other families that meet income and other eligibility requirements.

Figure 7 illustrates the expected demand for child care in Minnesota.

Reimbursement Incentives and Policies

Minnesota reimburses accredited providers up to 10 percent more than nonaccredited pro-

Figure 7.   Will Demand for Care Exceed Supply?

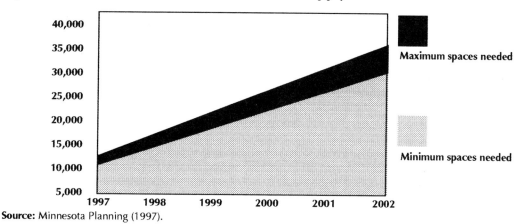

Source: Minnesota Planning (1997).

Minnesota's At-Home Infant Care Program

Minnesota passed the At-Home Infant Care bill in 1997, which will provide up to 12 monthly stipends for a parent to stay home to care for his or her infant. The parent must be income-eligible for the basic sliding fee program, and only one parent qualifies in a two-parent household. The level of assistance is 75 percent of the maximum reimbursement rate for family child care in the county of residence.

Source: Child Care Works, Minneapolis, Minnesota.

---

viders.[208] The state pays rates at the 75th percentile and maintains current rates by conducting annual market surveys.[209]

Parent Involvement and Family Support

Minnesota has experienced success with integrating child care initiatives and parent education within a family support structure. The state funds four early childhood family support programs that involve parents.

- Early Childhood Family Education (ECFE)—This program, offered through school districts, enhances the ability of all parents to provide for their children's optimal learning and development through education and support from birth to kindergarten. ECFE programs are locally planned and generally include parent discussion groups, play and learning activities for children, early screening and home visits. The state appropriated $29.7 million for the FY 1998-99 biennium to serve 283,000 children.[210]
- Learning Readiness—This program provides comprehensive services for children between the ages 3 1/2 to 5. Also locally planned, these programs include family literacy, health referrals, nutrition, parent involvement, a social services plan and community outreach. The state appropriated $20.7 million for the FY 1998-99 biennium to serve 47,000 children.
- Way to Grow—This community-based initiative emphasizes children and their families with the greatest need. It provides outreach to parents before their child's birth up to age 6 and helps them access resources through home visits and family resource centers. The state appropriated $950,000 for the FY 1998-99 biennium to serve 4,530 children.
- Head Start—As mentioned before, this federal program provides comprehensive prekindergarten services to children who are poor or have a disability. The state also funds an Early Head Start program to assist families of young children. The state appropriated $37.5 million in the FY 1998-99 biennium to serve 15,645 children.[211]

Minnesota appropriated more than $93 million for these and other family support programs in FY 1998 and FY 1999 (See pp. 26–28 for more information about family support programs.) Additional state resources will also be directed toward the school-age extended-day programs. A 1996 evaluation of low-income participants in ECFE found improved parental understanding of child development and how they relate to their child, as well as increased parent-child interaction. The evaluation also found that more lower-income parents in the program demonstrated an improved awareness of their child than they did changes in parenting behavior and role perception. A 1992 ECFE parent outcome study revealed higher levels of self-esteem and support than before and an improvement in children's social skills, self-confidence, and language and communication skills.[212]

Empowering Resource and Referrals to Help Providers and Parents

Minnesota has developed statewide benchmarks to monitor how many parents are satisfied with their child care. In the 1997 session, the Legislature approved a law to provide funding for resource and referral programs (R&Rs) for parent information and consultation, recruitment, and technical assistance and training for new providers. The new law encourages awards of these R&R grants to programs that provide child care during nonstandard hours, programs or providers that are seeking accreditation, and educational entities that offer scholarships and training to providers. To further assist and encourage providers, Minnesota enacted a student loan forgiveness program for child care workers. The law allows the loan to be forgiven if the participant provides child care for 12 months following the completion of courses paid for by the loan.[213]

Integrating Early Childhood Services into a Variety of Policies

Recognizing the important links between children's issues and education issues, the Minnesota Legislature reorganized the structures responsible for child and family issues in 1996 by creating a new state agency, the Department of Children, Families and Learning, and by consolidating legislative oversight of early childhood services. Several committees in the Legislature formerly recommended appropriations for various early childhood services. The Senate Crime Prevention Committee, for example, appropriated funds for Head Start and the Learning Readiness programs to prevent delinquency and crime.[214] Comparable legislative committees in both the Senate and House now have been formed and include three finance divisions: family and early childhood education, K-12 and higher education. With the exception of regulation, all child care issues now fall within the purview of these committees. The reorganization is an administrative effort to coordinate decisions for virtually all the state's programs and funding for young children. The Family and Early Childhood Education Division budget appropriated more than $393 million in FY 1998 and FY 1999 for a range of state programs. This appropriation represented a 58 percent increase over the previous biennium for these programs.[215]

For more information, contact: Barbara Yates, Assistant Commissioner, Minnesota Department of Children, Families and Learning, (612) 296-9010.

North Carolina

- Expanding a Successful Initiative
- Elements and Variations of Smart Start
- Linking Provider Education with Better Pay
- Innovative Financing to Expand and Improve Care

In 1993, the North Carolina legislature and governor approved Smart Start, an initiative to make early care and education services available to all children under age six. The initiative started with a dozen counties in 1993 and was expanded statewide in 1997. The state authorizes county partnerships to design and implement Smart Start to fit local needs. In 1997 legislators reemphasized that Smart Start should focus on child care-related activities by earmarking 70 percent of the funds for direct services. The law also allows an increased earmark of these funds for subsidies for children from low-income families, depending on counties' needs. The legislature, however, resisted attempts to give TANF children priority in receiving Smart Start services, maintaining that Smart Start is for all children from age birth to 5 years of age.

Demographic Information

1995 Population: 7,195,138*

1995 Child Population (under 18): 1,542,000*
Children under 18 as percent of population: 21.4%*
1995 Children under 5: 513,888*
1995 Poverty Rate (all people): 12.6%*

Poor Children under 6, 1990-1992: 138,154**
Children under 6 Poverty Rate, 1990-1992: 23.9%**

Number of Children under 18 with Working Parent(s): 1,086,801†
Percent of Children under 18 with Working Parent(s): 68%†

State Median Income: $44,582

Licensed Child Care Centers: 3,546

Licensed Family Child Care Providers: 4,466

Sources:
*1995 Census Bureau tables
**Map and Track, National Center for Children in Poverty, Appendix C
†Working Mother "State of the States," May 1996
(4-person family, fiscal year 1997), Federal Register 61, 54: 11213
Based on state reports, January 1997

Expanding a Successful Initiative

Smart Start gives counties flexible funds to implement locally-designed programs for families with young children. Funds are made available through a competitive grant process to county-based nonprofit partnership boards that include families, educators, nonprofit organizations, service providers and representatives of community groups. The initiative allows counties to choose from a range of comprehensive support services to enhance child care services.

A 1996 independent performance audit by Coopers and Lybrand found that Smart Start has improved the quality of early care and education, increased child care spaces and expanded children's access to medical services. It stated that the program "is an extremely ambitious early childhood and health initiative" and that it "delivers substantial good to children and families in the State of North Carolina."[216]

In the 1997 session, the legislature expanded Smart Start to include all 100 counties and increased state funding by 30 percent—or more than $22 million—to pay for the expansion and a number of quality improvements. Initially funded at $20 million per year, Smart Start funding has quintupled in five years to about $100 million in FY 1998. During the last two years, state policy makers directed the initiative to help low-income families in need of child care subsidies. In 1996, the legislature required that at least 30 percent of Smart Start's direct services money be used for child care subsidies and in 1997 the legislature authorized an increase in this minimum subsidy amount to 50 percent if needed.[217] In 1996 the legislature expanded poor families' access to child care by subsidizing families up to 75 percent of the SMI, up from approximately 47 percent. To raise eligibility and continue reimbursement rates at the current market rate, the legislature made changes to the state's sliding fee scale. Parent fees now range from 7 percent to 9 percent of a family's income, depending on its size. Under this new structure, welfare families that were exempt now will pay a fee. Some parent copayments are higher than in the past, generating the additional revenue to increase eligibility.[218] In 1997, legislators debated but ultimately rejected a transfer of a significant amount of TANF funds to Smart Start because they wanted to spend the funds for welfare reform and reasoned that Smart Start activities extend beyond these purposes.[219] Since its inception in 1993, the initiative has served 154,000 children, including child care subsidies for 34,000 children.[220]

Elements of Smart Start
Smart Start programs spend their nonsubsidy direct services funds in different ways. The primary areas that receive funding include:

- Child care quality
- Parent education and literacy
- Teacher education and support
- Health and nutritional initiatives
- Resource and referral
- Administration and evaluation
- Community outreach and awareness

Variations in Smart Start
Smart Start is an example of a state early childhood initiative that allows comprehensive services, including health care, parent education, voluntary home visits, counseling and other social services. Research and state experiences have shown that early childhood policies that are augmented with comprehensive services may produce better outcomes for children.[221] Several counties have chosen to emphasize health care services in their Smart Start programs. One county funds a nurse to provide regular health check-ups for children at child care centers and family day care homes. Another county developed a dental care kit for preschool children to use at child care centers. One county has a van for nurses to provide medical services in places such as child care facilities. The performance audit found improved coordinated health initiatives in 10 counties, noting that, "Overall, health initiatives funded by the partnerships seem to be creating healthier communities and making individuals more aware of what public services are available to them."[222]

Linking Provider Education with Better Pay
As part of Smart Start, the North Carolina legislature appropriated $1.4 million in FY 1998 to fund the TEACH (Teacher Education And Compensation Helps) project, which was initiated in 1993 with funding of $1 million per year.[223] TEACH links compensation to more education for providers, with a goal of reducing teacher turnover. The program provides scholarships so that early care and education practitioners can return to school. Scholarship recipients who complete their course work receive additional compensation in the form of a raise or bonus. Practitioners who receive TEACH scholarships make a commitment to stay at their center for a year after they complete their course work. Several other states have reproduced this program. North Carolina also is working to improve quality with a goal to increase the number of child care facilities that are nationally accredited.

Innovative Financing to Expand and Improve Care
North Carolina guarantees loans for start-up and expansion of child care facilities. The state invests funds with the Rural Center to guarantee loans, made by participating banks, to child care providers in 50 rural counties. In addition, the state transfers federal funds to the Center for Community Self-Help, an intermediary that issues loans from a revolving loan fund and provides technical assistance to providers. These loans from private, state and federal partners provide a viable source of capital for providers.[224]

For more information, contact: Mary Ellen Sylvester, North Carolina Legislative Fiscal Research Division, (919) 733-4910; or Sue Russell, Day Care Services Association, (919) 967-3272.

Ohio

- Head Start and Preschool
- Coordinating Head Start, Preschool and Child Care
- Comprehensive Services and Family Support
- Loan Programs

Ohio is among the nation's leaders in early childhood care and education financing and coordination. The legislature has been an integral part of efforts to expand services to all eligible children whose families are interested to coordinate preschool with child care, to coordinate Head Start services within the early childhood care and education system, and to provide comprehensive services to more families with young children.

Head Start and Preschool

The Ohio legislature has launched an ambitious policy to provide early childhood care and education opportunities to low-income children, using a two-fold strategy. The state appropriates substantial amounts of money to supplement Head Start and also funds a smaller, state-operated public school preschool program. This program also adheres to the federal Head Start performance standards. By supplementing and extending the federal Head Start infrastructure, the state can serve additional children in a program that has proven effective in preparing children for school. The purpose of funding a separate state preschool program is to maintain variety among providers, offer parental choice and serve additional children.[225]

Demographic Information

1995 Population: 11,150,506*
1995 Child Population (under 18): 3,004,000*
Children under 18 as percent of population: 26.9%*
1995 Children under 5: 772,833
1995 Poverty Rate (all people): 11.5%*

Poor Children under 6, 1990-1992: 195,108**
Children Under 6 Poverty Rate, 1990-1992: 19.8%**

Number of Children under 18 with Working Parent(s): 1,677,613†
Percent of Children under 18 with Working Parent(s): 60%†

State Median Income: $46,848

Licensed Child Care Centers: 3,717

Licensed Family Child Care Providers: 7,285
(including 6,998 certified [licensed] family child care providers and 1,287 certified relative family child care providers; based on state reports)

Sources:
* 1995 Census Bureau tables
** Map and Track, National Center for Children in Poverty, Appendix C
† Working Mother "State of the States," May 1996
(4-person family, fiscal year 1997), Federal Register 61, 54: 11213
Based on state reports

Ohio has committed to offer access to these services by 1999 to all Head Start eligible children whose families desire them with either Head Start or public school preschool funds in conjunction with child care funding. Legislators appropriated $83.7 million in state funds—in addition to Ohio's federal Head Start allocation—for fiscal year 1998 and $17.4 million for the state public school preschool program for FY 1998.[226] With an appropriation of approximately $145 million for Head Start and an additional $33 million for the state's public school preschool program during the 1996-97 biennium, 4,300 additional children received services and the state's coverage of eligible children increased to 80 percent.[227] With the new federal and state funds, Ohio will serve more than 60,000 children in Head Start alone. When combined with proposed public preschool funds, the state will serve about 88 percent of those eligible—the highest percentage in the nation. In addition, Ohio has included Head Start eligible children with disabilities in preschool, which increases the total percentage of eligible children served to 92 percent.[228]

Coordinating Head Start, Preschool and Child Care

As one of the first states to streamline its publicly-funded child care system, Ohio had experience with systems coordination. Subsequent to its coordinated child care funding law, the state

Figure 8. Ohio's Head Start Funding

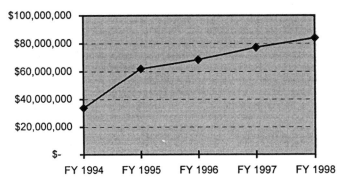

legislature linked child care with Head Start and public school preschool to address the needs of working families who need full-day, year-round care; Ohio children of working parents also benefit from these comprehensive services. Members of the Ohio House proposed to earmark 25 percent of state Head Start funds for full-day, wraparound care in 1993. Although the initiative failed that year, the legislature employed a strategy in 1995 that extended program hours for a variety of settings and providers. The 1995 budget earmarked $6 million per year during the 1996-97 biennium for full-day Head Start or public school preschool—$3 million was dedicated from the state-funded Head Start budget and $3 million came from the Job Opportunity and Basic Skills (JOBS, the federal job training and education program for welfare recipients under the former AFDC system) and child care budgets.[229] Although this earmark was folded into the state-funded Head Start continuation budget for the 1998-99 biennium, state decision makers have developed other strategies to accomplish coordinated services. For example, by 1995, the state departments of education and human services and the Head Start-Ohio Collaboration Project identified at least five specific models for collaboration between child care, Head Start, and other early childhood care and education programs that have been implemented locally (see box below).[230]

Ohio's Collaboration Options

1. *Enrollment in both Head Start or public school preschool and child care. Head Start or the public school preschool program provides transportation to and from the child care provider.*

2. *Enrollment in both Head Start or public school preschool and child care located in the same facility.*

3. *Child care or other early childhood providers are a delegate agency of Head Start, with the delegate required to meet Head Start program performance standards. Services are provided in the same location and the delegate agency is included in federal or state-funded Head Start review.*

4. *Head Start and public school preschool contract with a child care program in one location. The contract can specify program components, standards and hours of the child care provider, so a child may receive separate and different services.*

5. *Enhanced services that combine child care and Head Start and preschool without distinction. The services are delivered in a single setting as one program.*

Through these models, program roles and responsibilities become more integrated, increasing continuity of care and support for children and their families.

A recent legislative oversight report found that the collaboration has resulted in more families and children receiving services. Many groups in the state had success with collaboration efforts, including child care providers, providers serving children with disabilities or special needs, higher education, vocational schools and other social services agencies.[231]

Comprehensive Services and Family Support

Building on its success with Head Start, Ohio also established funding to increase services to children from birth to 3 years of age and their families to complement the recently-created federal Early Head Start program, which allocates about $120 million per year for programs to provide comprehensive national support and services to low-income families with children under age 3 and to pregnant women. Ohio appropriated $12 million for Early Start during 18 months in the FY 1996-97 budget and $19.7 million for the 1998-99 biennium, of which more than one-third is from TANF.[232]

Loan Programs

To help child care providers access capital, two Ohio agencies—the Department of Development and the Department of Human Services—established a Day Care Grant and Loan Program. This revolving loan fund makes micro-loans of up to $25,000 to start or expand family child care homes or centers. Loans are awarded for up to five years at a maximum interest rate of prime plus two percent. Resulting from this program are planning grants of up to $10,000 and technical assistance, administered by the Community Development Finance Fund, which are available to for-profit and nonprofit entities that want to start a program, including new construction or renovation.[233]

For more information, contact: Susan Rohrbaugh, Ohio Governor's Office, Families and Children First, Head Start-Ohio Collaboration Office, (614) 728-9433; Paul Frannholtz, Ohio Department of Human Services, (614) 752-6223; or Jane Wieckel, Ohio Department of Education, (614) 466-0224.

Oregon

- Goals for Serving All Children
- Serving Working Families
- Linking Child Care with Prekindergarten Programs and Head Start
- Benchmarks for Child Indicators
- Family Child Care and Relative Care

Since the late 1980s, Oregon legislators have persistently taken steps to develop early childhood services, including preschool and child care services for working families. Since 1987, Oregon's state-funded preschool program for three- and four-year-olds has emphasized a Head Start model.

Goals for Serving all Children

The state's early childhood efforts have been characterized by long-term planning and public-private partnerships. In the mid-1980s the legislature established the Oregon Commission for Child Care, which reports on the status of child care and proposes a legislative agenda each biennium. For the 1997-99 biennium the commission's financing task force will review finance, cost and fee issues and will recommend a legislative agenda for the 1999 session. The governor's Readiness to Learn Task Force plans a legislative agenda that expands the comprehensive preschool services. The legislative agenda includes targeting 50 percent of all eligible children to be served by 1999 and 100 percent of all eligible children by 2004.[234]

Serving Working Families

Since 1990, Oregon has emphasized employment-related child care services for the increasing number of families that are moving from welfare into work. The state uses no waiting list. Oregon has met program growth by investing funds, and now reinvests some TANF savings in child care as a result of reduced welfare caseloads. The state also has been increasing funds to support various community-based strategies to increase the availability of child care. Parent copayments were increased in 1996 to offset an increase in provider rates. The sliding fee scale is designed to target assistance to very low-income families.[235]

The state's reimbursement rates are considered to be low and copayments high. The state reimburses providers at the 75th percentile, but this level is based on a 1992 market rate survey. Copayments have been raised twice since 1990.[236] This poses a challenge for those who want working parents to use more professional child care providers. Market rate, consumer and provider surveys currently are being sponsored by the state to determine to what extent access to quality child care has been limited by the provider rates, and whether client self-sufficiency has been limited by the copayment structure.

The legislature expanded the state child care tax credit in 1997, which is available to families with incomes up to 200 percent of the FPL, as long as the family earns at least $6,000 annually.

This nonrefundable tax credit applies up to 40 percent of a family's child care expenses.[237] The tax credit can help families that lose eligibility for child care assistance.

Linking Child Care with Prekindergarten Programs and Head Start

Oregon initiated a preschool program in 1987; the program now serves approximately 30 percent of eligible children. Based on a Head Start model, the preschool program provides comprehensive services and is linked to the Head Start program through a collaborative process. Through a series of strategic planning processes initiated in 1990, state early childhood administrators developed child and family outcome measures for their child care and preschool programs. State law mandates that the preschool program use Head Start performance standards and eligibility requirements.[238] State and regional early care and education administrators have written collaborative agreements concerning service coordination and services to children with disabilities.[239] In the 1997 session legislators appropriated an additional $10 million per year to expand the preschool program. Oregon policy makers and federal Head Start officials are committed to support models that link Head Start and the state preschool program with child care to provide full-day services to working families.[240] Some programs blend Child Care and Development Block Grant funds with Head Start funds to offer full-day services, but discrepancies between the funding systems are challenging and careful analysis is needed to create solutions. Current collaborative agreements are central to the process of developing these solutions.

Oregon's Head Start collaboration project successfully worked with child care providers and others in the early childhood community to build strong, community-based services for families. The project has provided a child care-Head Start planning guide to help communities bring early care and education programs together.[241]

Benchmarks for Child Indicators

Oregon has adopted 92 benchmarks to focus efforts to improve the well-being of Oregon's children. Benchmarks must be comparable to an outside standard and flexible enough to adapt to changing conditions. The Oregon benchmarks measure families' well-being using social, economic and environmental health factors and are monitored by the state Progress Board. Some indicators of early childhood education and health are included in the benchmarks, such as children entering school ready to learn. The Oregon Progress Board and the Department of Education have developed a survey instrument for kindergarten teachers to use to measure children's readiness to learn. Results will be used to more effectively monitor progress on that benchmark. Data on related benchmarks report that childhood immunizations have risen drastically since 1991 and use of prenatal care has risen slightly. In addition, the Oregon legislature requires an annual report card on the status of schools, including preschools.[242]

Family Child Care and Relative Care

In 1993 the legislature enacted a law requiring family child care registration and in 1997 enacted a measure to improve health and safety in family child care homes.[243] Both the legislature and public-private partnerships have focused on improving family child care in particular. Since 1987, Oregon's family child care providers have participated in a series of public-private training and accreditation initiatives that reflect a pattern of improving family child care. Family child care providers are now electronically linked through an e-mail network that enhances their professional presence in the policy making process.[244]

About half of Oregon children who receive a state child care subsidy are in care that is exempt from regulation under state law. This includes care by friends and relatives.[245] All providers that receive a public subsidy must meet health and safety standards, including criminal and child protective service records checks. These requirements are equivalent to those for regulated providers. According to a consumer survey conducted for the state by Dr. Arthur Emlen in

1995, "...the pattern of care is quite similar to low-income child-care consumers and not all that dissimilar to all Oregon families who purchase child care."[246] The state is working with local child care resource and referral agencies to increase outreach to family child care providers—including those providers that are exempt from regulation—to improve the quality of care.[247]

With the assistance of corporate and philanthropic sponsors since the mid-1980s, Oregon providers also have participated in several initiatives focused on better care by:

• Providing for family child care accreditation;
• Providing a statewide training and professional development program for child care providers;
• Investing in the community supply of services;
• Developing innovative financing systems; and
• Establishing a statewide public engagement campaign, "Oregon's Child: Everyone's Business."[248]

One promising development in Oregon is a public-private partnership between child care R&R services and a network of community development organizations to expand child care in low-income housing developments and neighborhoods. Oregon involves parents in setting early childhood standards, and participating parents advocate for system change. The state has established an advisory committee comprised of parents and community representatives to help increase the parents' voice in decision making.[249]

For more information, contact: Linda Stern, Oregon Child Care Division, Employment Department (503) 947-1409; or Gayle McMurria-Bachik, Oregon Department of Education, (503) 378-5585 x662

CONCLUSION

State legislators are recognizing that investing in the first few years of life has important long-lasting implications for many policy areas, including the economy, education, welfare reform, criminal justice and health care. Child care and early education issues are central to this investment. Effective state policies result from thoughtful planning and consideration of trade-offs and consequences to help young children learn and develop in a healthy and safe way. Recent federal changes offer state lawmakers an opportunity to establish coordinated early childhood systems that help families of all income levels maintain employment and receive other family support services. At a recent White House conference on child care, President Clinton proposed several policies, including establishing pay incentives for providers who participate in more training, directing Americorps national service volunteers to care for school-age children and facilitating background checks for potential providers. As federal decision makers grapple with these and other proposals, state legislators across the political spectrum, who already have been at the forefront of the issue, will continue to develop child care policies that will shape the next generation.

NOTES

1. John M. Broder, "Clinton Pledges $300 Million Toward Improving Child Care," *New York Times,* October 24, 1997, A24.

2. Rima Shore, *Rethinking the Brain: New Insights into Early Development* (New York: Families and Work Institute, 1997), 27-29.

3. W. Steven Barnett, "Long-Term Effects of Early Childhood Programs on Cognitive and School Outcomes," *The Future of Children: Long-Term Outcomes of Early Childhood Programs* 5, no. 3 (Los Altos, Calif.: The Center for the Future of Children,The David and Lucille Packard Foundation, Winter 1995), 44-46; Hirokazu Yoshikawa, "Long-Term Effects of Early Childhood Programs on Social Outcomes and Delinquency," *The Future of Children,* 52.

4. Arlene Johnson, "The Business Case for Work-Family Programs," *Journal of Accountancy* 180, no. 2 (August 1995): 53-57.

5. *Report of the Colorado Business Commission on Child Care Financing* (Denver: State of Colorado, 1995), 7.

6. Susan Russell and Monica Rohacek, *Child Care Subsidy: An Investment Strategy for North Carolina* (Raleigh, N.C.: Day Care Services Association, 1996), 1.

7. Lawrence J. Schweinhart, Helen V. Barnes and David P. Weikart, *Significant Benefits: The High/Scope Perry Preschool Study Through Age 27* (Ypsilanti, Mich.: High/Scope Press, 1993), xviii.

8. William T. Gormley Jr., *Everybody's Children: Child Care as a Public Problem* (Washington, D.C.: The Brookings Institution, 1995), 98.

9. Richard W. Judy and Carol D'Amico, *Workforce 2020: Work and Workers in the 21st Century* (Indianapolis: Hudson Institute, 1997), 53; U.S. Department of Health and Human Services, Child Care Bureau and Maternal and Child Health Bureau, *Healthy Child Care America: Blueprint for Action* (Washington, D.C.: 1995), 1; Howard Hayghe, *Current Population Survey* (Washington, D.C.: Bureau of Labor Statistics, March 1994) Unpublished data; Donald J. Hernandez, "Changing Demographics: Past and Future Demands for Early Childhood Programs," *The Future of Children: Long-Term Outcomes of Early Childhood Programs* 5, no. 3 (Los Altos, Calif.: The Center for the Future of Children,The David and Lucille Packard Foundation, Winter 1995): 145-160.

10. "Married Moms More Likely to Work Full-Time: Study," *Report on Preschool Programs* (Business Publishers Inc., Silver Spring, Md., September 7, 1994, 177; Donald J. Hernandez, 151-152; "Enrollments Rise in South, But So Does Population," *Report on Preschool Programs,* April 2, 1997, 52.

11. Lynne M. Casper, "Who's Minding Our Preschoolers?" *Current Population Reports,* P70-53, (U.S. Bureau of the Census: March 1996), 2.

12. Ellen Galinsky, James T. Bond and Dana E. Friedman, *The Changing Workforce: Highlights of a National Study* (New York, N.Y.: Families and Work Institute: 1993), 65.

13. Shelley Smith, Mary Fairchild and Scott Groginsky, *Early Childhood Care and Education: An Investment That Works,* 2nd ed. (Denver, Colo.: National Conference of State Legislatures, 1997), 3.

14. Roger Neugebauer, "Child Care Demographics: Part I," *Child Care Information Exchange, Insider's Report #3* (Child Care Information Exchange, 1996), 2.

15. U.S. Department of Education, *National Study of Before and After School Programs*, Final Report (Portsmouth, N.H.: RMC Research Corporation, 1993), 15; U.S. Bureau of the Census, *Who's Minding the Kids? Child Care Arrangements: Fall 1991*, Current Population Reports, P70-36, (Washington, D.C., 1994), 13.

16. Data on child care expenses from *Child Care Information Exchange*, July 1996. Data collected from Resource and Referral agencies in each city. Data on average university costs cited in *Statistical Abstract of the United States 1994* (Washington, D.C.: U.S. Department of Commerce, 1994). Original data from The College Board, New York, Annual Survey of Colleges 1993 and the Boston Resource and Referral agency.

17. Lynne Casper, "What Does It Cost to Mind Our Preschoolers?" *Current Population Reports*, P70-52, (U.S. Bureau of the Census: September 1995), 4.

18. National Center for Children in Poverty, Columbia School of Public Health, *One in Four: America's Youngest Poor*, 6, 2 (New York: NCCP, Columbia School of Public Health, Winter 1996-1997), 1.

19. Nancy Ebb, *Child Care and Welfare Reform: More Painful Choices* (Washington, D.C.: Children's Defense Fund, 1995), 5.

20. U.S. General Accounting Office, *Poor Preschool-Aged Children: Numbers Increase but Most Not in Preschool*, (Washington, D.C.: U.S. GAO, July 1993), 2.

21. Center for Research on Women, School-Age Child Care Project, *I Wish the Kids Didn't Watch So Much TV: Out-of-School Time in Three Low-Income Communities* (Wellesley, Mass.: Wellesley College, Center for Research on Women, 1996), 7.

22. Cost, Quality and Outcomes Study Team, *Cost, Quality and Child Outcomes in Child Care Centers, Public Report*, 2nd ed. (Denver: University of Colorado at Denver, 1995), 17; Cost, Quality and Child Outcomes in Child Care Centers Datafile, (Denver: University of Colorado at Denver, Department of Economics). Available from ERIC Clearinghouse on Elementary and Early Childhood Education, Champaign, Ill.

23. Neugebauer, "Child Care Demographics, Part I," 2; CQO Study Team, *Cost, Quality and Child Outcomes, Public Report*, 26.

24. Ellen Galinsky et al., *The Study of Children in Family Child Care and Relative Care: Highlights of Findings* (New York: Families and Work Institute, 1994), 4.

25. "A Profile of the Child Care Work Force," *Child Care Bulletin* (National Child Care Information Center, Vienna, Va.) 16, (July/August 1997): 2; Marcy Whitebook, National Center for the Early Childhood Work Force, fax communication, October 27, 1997; Suzanne W. Helburn, ed., *Cost, Quality and Child Outcomes, Technical Report*, (Denver: Department of Economics, Center for Research in Economic and Social Policy, University of Colorado at Denver, 1995), 103; Marcy Whitebook, Deborah Phillips, and Carolee Howes, *National Child Care Staffing Study Revisited: Four Years in the Life of Center-Based Child Care* (Oakland, Calif.: Child Care Employee Project, 1993), 10.

26. Whitebook, fax communication.

27. CQO Study Team, *Cost, Quality and Child Outcomes, Public Report*, 45.

28. "A Profile of the Child Care Work Force," *Child Care Bulletin*, 2.

29. Sharon L. Kagan and Nancy E. Cohen, *Not By Chance: Creating an Early Care and Education System for America's Children* (New Haven, Conn.: Yale Bush Center in Child Development and Social Policy, The Quality 2000 Initiative, 1997, Executive Summary.

30. Carl Sussman, "Housing-Leveraged Facilities Finance: A Model for Child Care Centers," A paper prepared for the Local Initiatives Support Corporation for the National Child Care Initiative, November 7, 1996, 1.

31. John Morris, University of Colorado at Denver, telephone conversation, September 23, 1997.

32. Helburn, ed., *Cost, Quality and Child Outcomes in Child Care Centers: Technical Report*, 172.

33. Anne Mitchell, Louise Stoney and Harriet Dichter, *Financing Child Care in the United*

States: An Illustrative Catalog of Current Strategies (Kansas City, Missouri: Ewing Marion Kauffman Foundation and Philadelphia: The Pew Charitable Trusts, 1997), 97, 103.

34. National Conference of State Legislatures, *State Legislative Summary: Children, Youth, and Family Issues* (Denver, Colo.: NCSL, 1985-1996).

35. Maryland Department of Business and Economic Development, *DBED's Day Care Financing Programs,* April 1997; Joan Case, Maryland Business and Economic Development Department, telephone conversation, October 24, 1997; Bernard Johnston, "Ohio's Day Care Grant and Loan Program," *Child Care Bulletin,* (NCCIC, Vienna, Va.), 10, (July/August 1996), ericps.ed.uiuc.edu/nccic/ccb-ja96/ohio.html; World Wide Web; 1997 Conn. Acts., P. A. 0259, Sec. 12-18.

36. Mitchell et al., *Financing Child Care on the United States,* 106.

37. Maryland Business and Economic Development Department, *DBED's Day Care Financing Highlights,* April 1997; Case, telephone conversation; 1989 Ark. Acts, Act 202; 1985 Cal. Stats., Chap. 1440; 1997 Conn. Acts, P.A. 259; 1992 N.C. Sess. Laws, Chap. 900; 1989 Tenn. Pub. Acts, Chap. 420.

38. Mitchell et al., *Financing Child Care in the United States,* 99-101; Mae Hong, Illinois Facilities Fund, telephone conversation, September 3, 1997.

39. National Conference of State Legislatures, *State Legislative Summary: Children, Youth, and Family Issues.*

40. 1991 Md. Laws, Chap. 321; Arther J. Frankel et al., "Creating New Child Care Slots in Mini Child Care Centers: Big Bang for the Buck in New Jersey," *Children Today* 21, no. 1, 1992: 20-21; California Education Code, Section 8277.5-.6; 1997 Cal. AB 1542; Jack Hailey, California Senate Office of Research, e-mail, October 24, 1997.

41. Clay Springer, Hawaii Senate Ways and Means Committee, telephone conversation, October 8, 1996; 1990 Hawaii Acts, Act 334; 1985 Cal. Stats., Chap. 1026; Hailey, e-mail, October 23 and 30 1997; Center for Research on Women, National Institute on Out-of-School Time (formerly the School-Age Child Care Project), *School-Age Care Out of School Time,* Resource Notebook (Washington, D.C.: Child Care Bureau, March 1997), unnumbered.

42. Louise Stoney and Mark Greenberg, "The Financing of Child Care: Current and Emerging Trends," *The Future of Children: Financing Child Care,* 6, no. 2 (Los Altos, Calif., Center for the Future of Children, The David and Lucile Packard Foundation: 1996), 93.

43. 1996 Fla. Laws, Chap. 175, Sec. 85; Ron Cox, Florida Department of Children and Families, telephone conversation, July 10, 1997; Gail Richardson with Minerva Novero, *A Giant Step for Child Care: How the CCAC Indiana Symposium on Child Care Financing Launched Business-Community Initiatives* (New York: Child Care Action Campaign, undated), 1; State of Colorado, *Report of the Colorado Business Commission;* 1997 Hawaii Sess. Laws, Act 77; Mitchell, et al., *Financing Child Care in the United States,* 72, 79-80, 84-85.

44. National Conference of State Legislatures, *State Legislative Summary: Children, Youth, and Family Issues.*

45. 1995 Ark. Acts, Act 850; 1993 Ark. Acts, Act 820; 1994 Cal. Stats, Chap. 748; 1996 Conn. Acts, Act 262, Sec. 7; 1985 Fla. Laws, Chap. 85-118; 1995 Md. Laws, Chap. 492; 1996 Md. Laws, Chap. 109; 1987 Or. Laws, Chap. 682; 1994 R.I. Pub. Laws, Chap. 262.

46. Gwen Morgan, Center for Career Development in Early Care and Education, fax communication, October 19, 1997; Child Care Action Campaign, *Employer Tax Credits for Child Care: Asset or Liability?* (New York: CCAC, November 1989), v.

47. National Conference of State Legislatures, *Fiscal Program Sampling* (Denver: NCSL, 1996).

48. Morgan, telephone conversation, October 29, 1997.

49. 1995 Or. Laws, Chap. 685.

50. Helburn, ed., *Cost, Quality and Child Outcomes, Technical Report,* 1.

51. Galinsky et al., *The Study of Children in Family Child Care and Relative Care,* 4.

52. Shore, *Rethinking the Brain,* 30-31.

53. CQO Study Team, *Cost, Quality and Child Outcomes, Public Report*, 38.

54. Ibid., 33-35.

55. Helburn, ed., *Cost, Quality and Child Outcomes, Technical Report*, 1; National Center for the Early Childhood Work Force, "New Study Shows Better Teacher Compensation Plus NAEYC Accreditation Equals High Quality Child Care," April 16, 1997, press release.

56. CQO Study Team, *Cost, Quality and Child Outcomes, Public Report*, 38; Galinsky et al., *The Study of Children in Family Child Care and Relative Care*, 47-51.

57. The Children's Foundation, *1997 Child Care Center Licensing Study* (Washington, D.C.: The Children's Foundation, 1997).

58. Morgan, fax communication.

59. 1996 Colo. Sess. Laws, Chap. 63; Nancy Von Bargen, Oklahoma Office of Child Care, fax communication, October 30, 1997; 1997 Conn. Acts, P.A. 259, Sec. 11; 1997 Tex. Gen. Laws, H.B. 1555; Richard Fiene, Pennsylvania State University at Harrisburg, telephone conversation, October 16, 1997.

60. CQO Study Team, *Cost, Quality and Child Outcomes, Public Report*, 33.

61. 1993 N.C. Sess. Laws, Chap. 321, Sec. 254.

62. Carollee Howes, Ellen Smith and Ellen Galinsky, *The Florida Child Care Quality Improvement Study* (New York: Families and Work Institute, 1995), 17-18.

63. National Center for Missing And Exploited Children, *State Criminal History Background Check Laws—Amendments and New Laws, 1995 Session* (Arlington, Va.: NCMEC, 1995).

64. Morgan, fax communication.

65. 1997 Ark. Acts, Act 1198; Ark. Code Annotated, 20-78-602, 20-78-210; 1991 Cal. Stats., Chap. 660; Patty Siegel, *Trustline and California's Registration Process for License Exempt Child Care Providers* (San Francisco: California Child Care Resource and Referral Network, December 2, 1993); Or. Rev. Stat. Chap. 657.A.030 (1997).

66. CQO Study Team, *Cost, Quality and Child Outcomes, Public Report*, 38-39; Schweinhart et al., *Significant Benefits*, 235-238.

67. Sue Bredekamp and Stephanie Glowacki, "The First Decade of NAEYC Accreditation: Growth and Impact on the Field," *NAEYC Accreditation: A Decade of Learning and the Years Ahead* (Washington, D.C.: NAEYC, 1996), 8.

68. 1996 Fla. Laws, Chap. 175, Sec. 85.

69. Children's Defense Fund, *State Child Care Developments* (forthcoming).

70. Helburn, ed., *Cost, Quality and Child Outcomes, Technical Report*, 15-18.

71. Deborah Phillips and Anne Bridgman, eds. *New Findings on Children, Families, and Economic Self-Sufficiency: Summary of A Research Briefing* (Washington, D.C.: National Academy Press, 1995), 18.

72. CQO Study Team, *Cost, Quality and Child Outcomes, Public Report*, 35.

73. "Questions and Answers about Director Credentialing Efforts," *Taking the Lead: Director Credentialing*, The Center for Career Development in Early Care and Education at Wheelock College, http://ericps.crc.uiuc.edu/ccdece/ccdede.html; World Wide Web.

74. California Education Code, Section 8360.1 applies to administrators who have a direct contract with the state Department of Education to enroll subsidized children; Center for Career Development in Early Care and Education, "Child Care Licensing Requirements: Minimum Pre-Service Training, Annual Ongoing, and Administrative Training Hours for Directors in Child Care Centers," (Boston, Mass.: Wheelock College, Center for Career Development in Early Care and Education, June 11, 1997).

75. CQO Study Team, *Cost, Quality and Child Outcomes, Public Report*, 37.

76. Shore, *Rethinking the Brain*, Executive Summary, 14.

77. CQO Study Team, *Cost, Quality and Child Outcomes, Executive Summary*, 4.

78. CQO Study Team, *Cost, Quality and Child Outcomes, Public Report*, 37.

79. Diane Adams, Ruth Anne Foote, and Yasmina S. Vinci, *Making Child Care Work, A Study of Child Care Resource and Referral In the United States* (Washington, D.C.: National Association for Child Care Resource and Referral Agencies, 1996), 14.

80. Louise Stoney, *Giving Children a Strong Start: Effective Early Childhood Policy in the States* (Denver, Colo.: Education Commission of the States, 1997), 18.

81. First Impressions, *Colorado's Early Childhood Professional Credentialing System* (Denver, Colo.: Colorado Departments of Education and Human Services, April 1997), Preface.

82. Ruth Singer, New York State Child Care Coordinating Council, telephone conversation, July 18, 1997; 1997 N.Y. Laws, S. 5788.

83. 1997 Conn. Acts, Act 259; Von Bargen, fax communication; Commonwealth of Massachusetts, FY 98 Budget, Office of Child Care Services, 4130-3100; 1997 Mich. SB 169, Sec. 523.

84. "California: Helping Welfare Recipients to Pursue Careers in the Child Care Field," *Child Care Bulletin* (NCCIC, Child Care Bureau, Administration for Children and Families, U.S. Department of Health and Human Services, Vienna, Va.) 16, (July/August 1997): 6; 1996 Colo. Sess. Laws, Chap. 221; Child Care Law Center, *Recruiting Welfare Recipients for Child Care Work: Not A Panacea* (San Francisco, Calif.: Child Care Law Center, March 1996), 15-19.

85. "A Profile of the Child Care Work Force," *Child Care Bulletin*, 2.

86. CQO Study Team, *Cost Quality and Child Outcomes: Executive Summary; The Economics of Family Child Care* (Wheelock College: Forthcoming);"A Profile of the Child Care Work Force," *Child Care Bulletin*, 2.

87. Broder, "Clinton Pledges $300 Million Toward Improving Child Care," A24.

88. 1993 N.C. Sess. Laws, Chap. 561; Mary Ellen Sylvester, North Carolina Fiscal Research, "Summary of Smart Start Legislation, 1997-99 Regular Session," September 18, 1997.

89. Day Care Services Association, "T.E.A.C.H. Early Childhood Project," (North Carolina: Day Care Services Association, no date), 1-2.

90. "T.E.A.C.H. Project Helps Promote Professional Development in Six States," *Child Care Bulletin* (NCCIC, Child Care Bureau, Administration for Children and Families, U.S. Department of Health and Human Services, Vienna, Va.) 16, (July/August 1997): 7.

91. 1993 Ill. Laws, P.A. 432; 1993 Pa. Laws, Act 73; 1997 Minn. Laws, Chap. 162, Sec. 43; Cynthia Beal, River Valley Child Development Services, fax communication of "Apprenticeship For Child Development Specialists," November 13, 1997; 1996 R.I. Pub. Laws, Chap. 129, Sec. 18.

92. Children's Defense Fund, "1996 State and Selected Local Early Care and Education Developments," memorandum (Washington, D.C.: CDF, 1996), 2, 11.

93. Adams et al., *Making Child Care Work*, 38.

94. 1997 Ill. Laws, Act 507, Sec. 5.15; 1997 Minn. Laws, Chap 162, Secs. 46-47, 52, 61; Patty Siegel, California Child Care Resource and Referral Network, telephone conversation, October 15, 1997; Elizabeth Bonbright Thompson, Washington State Child Care Resource and Referral Network, telephone conversation and fax communication, October 14 and 15, 1997.

95. Schweinhart et al., *Significant Benefits*, 233-235.

96. Gina Adams and Jodi Sandfort, *First Steps, Promising Futures, Executive Summary*, (Washington, D.C.: Children's Defense Fund, 1994), 3, 5.

97. "Study Seeks to Debunk Head Start 'Fadeout'," *Report on Preschool Programs*, June 26, 1996, 98.

98. U.S. General Accounting Office, *Poor Preschool-Aged Children: Numbers Increase but Most Not in Preschool* (Washington, D.C.: U.S. GAO, July 1993), 2; Craig Turner, U.S. Head Start Bureau, telephone conversation, February 1995.

99. National Education Goals Panel, *Data Volume for the National Education Goals Report Volume 1: National Data* (Washington, D.C.: Government Printing Office, 1995).

100. *The Head Start State Collaboration Projects: Building Partnerships for the 21st Century* (Washington, D.C.: A handbook prepared by the federal Head Start staff, June 1997) 2.

101. Morgan, fax communication.

102. Georgia State University, Department of Early Childhood Education, *Georgia Prekindergarten Evaluation* (Atlanta: Georgia State University, September 1996), 1-2; Debbie Schumacher, Kentucky Department of Education, telephone conversations, August 17, 1994

and October 11, 1996; *KERA 1990-93 Preschool Results* (Frankfort, Ky.: Department of Education); Mary Frost, Washington Department of Community Development, telephone conversation, August 1994; Jennifer Priddy and Laura Walkush, *1992 ECEAP Longitudinal Study and Annual Report* (Olympia, Wash.: Washington Department of Community Development, 1993); Ed Schmidt, Connecticut House Democrats, fax communication, October 20, 1997; 1997 Conn. Acts, Act 259; Linda McCart, Ohio Governor's Family and Children First Office, telephone conversation, July 24, 1997.

103. Nancy DeRoberts Moore, Ohio Department of Education, telephone conversation, October 21, 1996; Ohio Legislative Office of Education Oversight, *Implementation of Head Start in Ohio* (Columbus, Ohio: LOEO, April 1997), 7; 1997 Conn. Acts, Act 259; 1997 Colo. Sess. Laws, SB 174; 1996 Fla. Laws, Chap. 175, Secs. 57-58, 78.

104. August 1997 handouts from Minn. Sen. Pat Piper, "Minnesota's Family and Early Childhood Education Budget Division - Selected Programs," and "Minnesota's Family & Early Childhood Education Budget - 1998-99"; Tennessee Select Committee on Children and Youth, *1994 Annual Report on Children's Initiatives* (June 9, 1994), 2,6; 1997 Hawaii Sess. Laws, Act 77.

105. 1997 Conn. Acts, Act 259; 1997 Colo. Sess. Laws, SB 174; 1993 N.C. Laws, Chap. 321, Sec. 254; 1997 Okla. HB 2170, Sec. 20, Part B4; Claudia San Pedro, Oklahoma Senate Staff, telephone conversation, November 12, 1997; Research and Evaluation: "Kentucky Looks at the First Year of Its Statewide Program and Charts a Course for the Future," *Family Resource Coalition Report* 12, nos. 3 and 4, Family Support and School-Linked Services (Fall/Winter 1993): 47; Kentucky Department of Education, *KERA Preschool 1990-93 Results*.

106. Senator Pat Piper, "Minnesota's Family and Early Childhood Education Budget Division - Selected Programs," handout; Marsha R. Mueller, Mueller Associates, LLC, for the Family Education Resources of Minnesota and the Minnesota Department of Children, Families and Learning, *Immediate Outcomes of Lower-Income Participants in Minnesota's Universal Access Early Childhood Family Education, Summary,* (Minneapolis, Minn., April 1996), 2; Minnesota Department of Education, *Changing Times, Changing Families, Minnesota Early Childhood Family Education: Parent Outcome Interview Study Summary* (St. Paul, Minn.: March 1992), 5.

107. "Healthy Growth for Hawaii's 'Healthy Start': Toward a Systematic Statewide Approach to the Prevention of Child Abuse and Neglect," *Zero to Three,* April 1991, 20; 1996 Fla. Laws, Chap. 175, Sec. 73.

108. Illinois Department of Human Services, "Child Care in Illinois" (Illinois Department of Human Services, Division of Family Support Services, Child Care and Development Section, Chicago, July 18, 1997, fact sheet); Dave Edie, Wisconsin Office of Child Care, telephone conversation, June 30, 1997; 1997 Vt. Acts, Act 178, Sec. 146; Kim Kaiser, Vermont Department of Social and Rehabilitation Services, fax communication, October 20, 1997; 1997 Colo. Sess. Laws, Chap. 120, Part 8, Sec. 1; Oxana Golden, Colorado Division of Child Care, Department of Human Services, fax communication, October 21, 1997; Department of Human Services, Office of the Director, "Rhode Island Child Care Fact Sheet," fax communication, July 18, 1997.

109. Children's Defense Fund, *State Child Care Developments* (forthcoming).

110. Troy Vick, Minnesota Child Care Assistance Program, Office of Children, Families and Learning, telephone conversation, July 31, 1997.

111. Mary Ellen Sylvester, North Carolina Legislative Fiscal Research Division, telephone conversation, September 15, 1997.

112. Children's Defense Fund, *State Child Care Developments* (forthcoming).

113. Larry Pintacuda, Florida Department of Children and Families, telephone conversation, October 2, 1997.

114. Administration for Children and Families, U.S. Department of Health and Human Services, *Change in Welfare Caseloads,* revised August 1997, obtained from http://www.acf.dhhs.gov/news/caseload.htm; World Wide Web.

115. Associated Press, "Clinton Tells States to Hit Welfare Goals," *Richmond Times-Dispatch,* September 30, 1997.

116. American Public Welfare Association, "The Child Care Challenge: States Leading the Way" (Washington, D.C.: APWA, August 1997), 2.

117. Edie, telephone conversation, July 3, 1997; Administration for Children and Families, *Change in Welfare Caseloads;* Judith Havemann and Barbara Vobjeda, "Wisconsin Moves to Cover Welfare's Day-Care Costs," *Washington Post,* December 13, 1996; obtained from washingtonpost.com; Internet.

118. Children's Defense Fund, *State Child Care Developments* (forthcoming); APWA, "The Child Care Challenge," 6, 9, 12; 1996 Iowa Acts, Chap. 1213.

119. Gina Adams and Nicole Oxendine Poersch, *1997 Edition Key Facts About Child Care and Early Education: A Briefing Book,* (Washington, D.C.: Children's Defense Fund, 1997) G-3.

120. Jack Hailey, California Senate Research, "Age of Child Whose Mother is Exempt from work Requirements," July 21, 1997; Children's Defense Fund, *State Child Care Developments* (forthcoming).

121. Hailey, "Age of Child Whose Mother is Exempt from Work Requirements," July 21, 1997.

122. Pat Urzedowski, Nebraska Health and Human Services System, telephone conversation, October 17, 1997.

123. Don Kassar, Iowa Department of Human Services, telephone conversation, July 18, 1997.

124. Anne Webers, Iowa Economic Assistance Department, telephone conversation, July 24, 1997, about the "Summary of Mathematica Policy Research Inc.," Annual Reports On the Evaluation of Iowa's Welfare Reform, (Des Moines, Iowa: February 5, 1996).

125. Mitchell et al., 29-32.

126. Pennsylvania Child Care Campaign, A Coalition of Parents, Child Care Providers, and Child Advocates, *Comments on DPW's Proposed Child Care Regulations,* (October 6, 1997), 5-6.

127. Casper, "What Does it Cost?," 4.

128. U.S. Department of Health and Human Services, *Federal Register* 62, 141, Proposed Rules, July 23, 1997, 39626.

129. Administration for Children and Families, *Child Care at the Crossroads: A Call For Comprehensive State and Local Planning* (Washington, D.C.: ACF, December 1996).

130. Casper, "What Does it Cost?," 4.

131. Elaine Kisker and Christine Ross, "Arranging Child Care," *The Future of Children: Welfare to Work* 7, no. 1, Center for the Future of Children (Los Altos, Calif.: The David and Lucile Packard Foundation, Spring 1997), 100.

132. Michele Piel, telephone conversation, September 19, 1997; Illinois Sliding Fee Scale.

133. Havemann and Vobjeda, "Wisconsin Moves to Cover Welfare's Day-Care Costs," A02; Kay Hendon, Wisconsin Office of Child Care, telephone conversation, February 7, 1997; "New W-2 Child Care Copay Schedule and Supply Building Initiative: Child Care Work Group Recommendation, Approved by the Governor," factsheet, December 12, 1996.

134. Teresa Vast, telephone conversation, October 29, 1997, and fax communication, October 30, 1997.

135. APWA, "The Child Care Challenge," 6-7, 9-10.

136. APWA, "The Child Care Challenge," 6, 9-10; Hailey, *California's Approach to Parent Fee Schedules,* August 1997, 1; Urzedowski, telephone conversation, July 18, 1997.

137. APWA, "The Child Care Challenge," 2.

138. Philadelphia Citizens for Children and Youth, Community Justice Project, *Parent Fees: State Examples Incorporating a Cost of Care Approach,* 1997.

139. U.S. Department of Health and Human Services, *Federal Register* 62, 141, Proposed Rules, July 23, 1997, 39626.

140. *Child Care System Under CAL-Works,* (Sacramento, CA: CDPAC), 3.

141. Nancy Ebb, Children's Defense Fund, testimony before the U.S. House Committee on Ways and Means, March 11, 1993.

142. Children's Defense Fund, *State Child Care Developments* (forthcoming); Janice Axelrod, Massachusetts Child Care Services, telephone conversation, September 25, 1997; Lewis Randolph, Tennessee Department of Human Services, telephone conversation, July 14, 1997.

143. 1997 Conn. Acts, Act 259; Children's Defense Fund, *State Child Care Developments* (forthcoming); Minn. Stats., 119B.13, Subdivision 2; Dave Edie, Wisconsin Office of Child Care, Department of Health and Social Services, and Edna Ranck, New Jersey Department of Human Services, Child Care Action Campaign Audioconference, *Innovative Ideas for Increasing Quality in Child Care,* November 17, 1997.

144. Children's Defense Fund, *State Child Care Developments* (forthcoming); 1993 Me. Laws, Chap. 158; 1991 Ohio Laws, H. 155.

145. 1996 Fla. Laws, Chap. 175, Sec. 78; APWA "The Child Care Challenge," 10; Children's Defense Fund, *State Child Care Developments* (forthcoming); 1995 Wis. Laws, Act 289.

146. 1997 Colo. Laws, SB 120; Children's Defense Fund, *State Child Care Developments* (forthcoming).

147. "Child Care Initiatives in the States," *Public Welfare,* (Washington, D.C.: APWA, Fall 1995), 45; APWA "The Child Care Challenge," 8, 10; 1997 Minn. Laws, Chap. 162, Sec. 52.

148. 1997 Ill. Laws, HB 635; Children's Defense Fund, *State Child Care Developments* (forthcoming).

149. 1996 Iowa Acts, Chap. 1213, Sec. 6; Children's Defense Fund, *State Child Care Developments* (forthcoming).

150. Carole Ponto, Rhode Island Department of Human Services, telephone conversation, July 31, 1997; Department of Human Services, "Rhode Island Child Care Fact Sheet," 2; Hailey, telephone conversation, October 6, 1994; Axelrod, telephone conversation; Carol Palmeroy, Vermont Department of Social and Rehabilitative Services, Child Care Services Division, telephone conversation, July 10, 1997; 1997 Colo. Laws, SB 120; *County Rate Increases Effective January 1, 1997,* Department of Human Services, Division of Child Care, 1997; 1995 Neb. Laws, LB 455, Sec. 20; Scott Groginsky, *Child Care and the Transition off Welfare,* (Denver: National Conference of State Legislatures, 1996).

151. Helen Blank, Children's Defense Fund, telephone conversation, November 26, 1996; 1997 Vt. Acts, Act 61, Section 159.

152. California Education Code, Secs. 8203, 8240, 8288, 8360.

153. 1993 Me. Laws, Chap. 158.

154. Louise Stoney, *Cash Payments for Child Care and the Child Care Disregard,* handout for CDF Workshop, 1996.

155. Ibid.

156. Children's Defense Fund, *State Child Care Developments* (forthcoming).

157. "Helping Families Work: Alternatives To The Child Care Disregard," *Working for Change* (San Francisco, Calif.: The Child Care Law Center, August 1994), 13, 20; Rhonda Present, Chicago JOBS Council, telephone conversation, May 30, 1996.

158. 1997 Cal. Stats., AB 107, California's 1997-98 budget, items 5180-196-0001, 5180-196-0890, 6110-196-0001, and 6110-196-0890.

159. 1997 Cal. Stats., AB 107, California's 1997-98 budget, item 6110-485(a), 2240-013-0001, 2240-013-0474, 2240-014-0001, and 2240-014-0472.

160. California Education Code, sections 8203, 8240, 8288, and 8360.

161. Hailey, fax communication, August 26, 1997.

162. California Education Code, section 8263(e).

163. 1997 Colo. Sess. Laws, Chap. 120, Part 8, Sec. 1; Golden, fax communication.

164. 1997 Colo. Sess. Laws, Chap. 120, Part 8, Sec. 1; Grace Hardy, Colorado Division of

Child Care, Department of Human Services, telephone conversation, June 2, 1997; County Rate Increases Effective 1/1/97, Colorado Division of Child Care, Department of Human Services.

165. 1997 Colo. Sess. Laws, Chap. 120.

166. 1997 Colo. Sess. Laws, Chap. 174.

167. 1996 Colo. Sess. Laws, Chap. 219.

168. Dayna Ashley-Oehm, Colorado Joint Budget Committee, telephone conversation, September 3, 1997.

169. Kathleen Shindler, Colorado Governor Roy Romer's Office, May 16, 1997, memorandum.

170. 1996 Colo. Sess. Laws, Chap. 221.

171. 1996 Colo. Sess. Laws, Chap. 63, Secs. 2-5

172. 1996 Colo. Sess. Laws, Chap. 220; Colorado Children's Campaign, October 15, 1997, letter.

173. Schmidt, fax communication.

174. Anne M. Hamilton, "New State Program Will Expand Preschool," *The Hartford Courant,* October 17, 1997, http://news.courant.com/article/ctnews8.stm; Internet.

175. Connecticut Commission on Children, "Preschool Bill 5461 - LCO 6052," memorandum, June 5, 1997; Schmidt, fax communication.

176. 1995 Conn. Acts, P.A. 266, Sec. 3; 1996 Conn. Acts, P.A. 262, Sec. 4.

177. 1996 Conn. Acts, Act 262, Sec. 8.

178. Connecticut Commission on Children, "Preschool Bill 5461 - LCO 6052," memorandum; 1996 Conn. Acts, Act 262, Secs. 1,7.

179. Connecticut Commission on Children, "Preschool Bill 5461 - LCO 6052," memorandum.

180. Paul Belcher, Florida Governor's Office of Planning and Budgeting, telephone conversations, June 30, 1997, and July 22, 1997; Pintacuda, telephone conversation.

181. Mitchell et al., *Financing Child Care in the United States,* 11-13.

182. Cox, telephone conversation, July 18, 1997.

183. Mitchell et al., *Financing Child Care in the United States,* 75-76.

184. 1996 Fla. Laws, Chap. 175, Sec. 85; Cox, telephone conversation.

185. Warren Eldridge, Florida Children's Forum, telephone conversation, September 25, 1997; *The Child Care Focus* (newsletter published by the Florida Children's Forum) 1, no. 2, July 1997, 5; 1996 Fla. Laws, Chap. 175, Sec. 85.

186. 1996 Fla. Laws, Chap. 175, Secs. 57-58.

187. 1991 Fla. Laws, Chap. 300; 1991 Fla. Laws, Chap. 266.

188. Howes et al., *The Florida Child Care Quality Improvement Study,* 1-2.

189. 1996 Fla. Laws, Chap. 175, Sec. 72.

190. Eldridge, telephone conversation, October 21, 1997.

191. 1996 Fla. Laws, Chap. 175, Secs. 56, 80.

192. 1996 Fla. Laws, Chap. 175, Sec. 73.

193. Illinois Department of Human Services, "Child Care in Illinois."

194. "Wiping Out the Waiting List," *Chicago Tribune,* June 30, 1997, 8, sec. 1.

195. Piel, telephone conversation, September 23, 1997.

196. "Wiping Out the Waiting List," *Chicago Tribune,* 8, sec. 1.

197. Piel, telephone conversation, September 19, 1997.

198. Richard Martin, Illinois Department of Human Services, telephone conversation, September 23, 1997.

199. Melita Marie Garcia, "Low-Income Day-Care Fees Under Scrutiny," *Chicago Tribune,* October 19, 1997, file:\\SCRUFFY\SHARE\Public Affairs\Clippings\October 97\Oct 20\IL; Internet.

200. Piel, telephone conversation, October 30, 1997.

201. "Helping Families Work: Alternatives to the Child Care Disregard," *Working for Change,* 13, 20.

202. Present, telephone conversation.

203. Piel, telephone conversation, February 18, 1997; Helen Blank, Children's Defense Fund, "Illinois Sets a Marker," memorandum, July 3, 1997.

204. Jan Stokely and Emily Heumann, *Child Care Bulletin,* July/August 1996, Issue 10, ericps.ed.uiuc.edu/nccic/ccb-ja96/ohio.html.; Hong, telephone conversation.

205. 1993 Ill. Laws, P.A. 88-432; Dan Bellm et al., *Making Work Pay in the Child Care Industry, Promising Practices for Improving Compensation,* (Washington, D.C.: National Center for the Early Childhood Work Force, 1997), 34; Illinois Department of Human Services, "Child Care in Illinois."

206. Senator Pat Piper, "Minnesota's Family and Early Childhood Education Budget - 1998-99," handout.

207. Vick, telephone conversations, July 22 and 31, 1997.

208. Minn. Stats., 119B.13, Subd. 2.

209. Cherie Kotilinek, Department of Children, Families, and Learning, telephone conversation, October 30, 1997.

210. Kotilinek, fax communication, October 8, 1997.

211. Senator Pat Piper, "Minnesota's Family and Early Childhood Education Budget Division—Selected Programs," handout.

212. Mueller, *Immediate Outcomes of Lower-Income Participants,* 2; Minnesota Department of Education, *Changing Times, Changing Families,* 5.

213. 1997 Minn. Laws, Chap. 162, Secs. 43, 46-47, 52.

214. Scott Groginsky and Jay Kroshus, "An Ounce of Prevention," *State Legislatures,* May 1995, 21.

215. Cynthia Coronado, Minnesota House of Representatives, Fiscal Analysis Department, telephone conversation, October 8, 1997.

216. "Coopers and Lybrand Performance Audit Gives Smart Start Solid Report Card," (North Carolina: NC Partnership for Children, April 23, 1996), Press Release, 2; Coopers and Lybrand, *State of North Carolina Smart Start Program Performance Audit, Final Report* (Chapel Hill, N.C.: Coopers and Lybrand, April 1, 1996), i.

217. Sylvester, *Summary of Smart Start Legislation, 1997-99 Regular Session*; Sylvester, memorandum, April 28, 1997 and fax communication, July 1, 1997.

218. Stephanie Fanjul, North Carolina Division of Child Development, telephone conversation, July 17, 1997.

219. Sylvester, telephone conversation, October 15, 1997.

220. Karen Hammonds-Blanks, North Carolina Legislative Fiscal Research Division, telephone conversation, September 24, 1997.

221. Smith et al., *Early Childhood Care and Education,* 82-84.

222. Coopers and Lybrand, *State of North Carolina Smart Start Program Performance Audit,* 63-67.

223. Sylvester, *Summary of Smart Start Legislation, 1997-99 Regular Session.*

224. Mitchell et al., *Financing Child Care in the United States,* 108-109; Sylvester, fax communication, October 28, 1997.

225. Smith et al., *Early Childhood Care and Education,* 24.

226. Susan Rohrbaugh, Ohio Governor's Family and Children First Office, fax communication, October 29, 1997.

227. Jerry Scott, Ohio Department of Education, telephone conversation, November 20, 1996.

228. Rohrbaugh, fax communication.

229. Smith et al., *Early Childhood Care and Education,* 24; DeRoberts-Moore, telephone conversation.

230. *Forging the Link, Child Care, Head Start and Education Partnerships Service Delivery Options* (Columbus: Head Start-Ohio Collaboration Office and the Ohio Department of Education, Division of Early Childhood Education, November 1995).

231. Ohio Legislative Office of Education Oversight, *Implementation of Head Start in Ohio,* (Columbus, Ohio: LOEO, April 1997), 20-21.

232. McCart, telephone conversation.

233. Bernard Johnston, "Ohio's Day Care Grant and Loan Program," *Child Care Bulletin,* July/August 1996, Issue 10, ericps.ed.uiuc.edu/nccic/ccb-ja96/ohio.html; Internet; Rohrbaugh, fax communication, October 28, 1997.

234. Gayle McMurria-Bachik, Oregon Department of Education, telephone conversation, October 8, 1997.

235. Larry Shadbolt, Oregon Adult and Family Services Division, Policy and Budget Section, fax communication, October 29, 1997.

236. Alvin Damm, Oregon Adult and Family Services, telephone conversation, October 21, 1997.

237. 1997 Or. Laws, Chap. 692.

238. Smith et al., *Early Childhood Care and Education,* 13-14.

239. Inter-Governmental Agreement between the Oregon Department of Education Early Intervention/Early Childhood Special Education and Region 10 Administration for Children and Families: Head Start Bureau for Services for Children with Disability Age Birth to School-Age, October 1997.

240. McMurria-Bachik, telephone conversation.

241. "Cooperation, Coordination, and Collaboration; A Guide for Child Care and Head Start Programs," Oregon Head Start Collaboration Project, revised October 1996.

242. McMurria-Bachik, telephone conversation.

243. 1993 Or. Laws, Chap. 733; 1997 Or. Laws, 399.

244. Janis Elliot, Oregon Child Care Division, Department of Employment, telephone conversation, August 20, 1997.

245. Ibid.

246. Arthur Emlen and Associates Inc., unpublished report of a consumer survey by the Oregon Adult and Family Services Division, July 1995.

247. Shadbolt, fax communication, November 5, 1997.

248. Elliot, telephone conversation.

249. Forging the Link Project, *Essential Elements of Programs for Children,* Draft, (Salem, Ore.: Oregon Department of Education, March 24, 1996), 5.

RESOURCE LIST

List of National Early Childhood Organizations

Bush Center in Child Development and Social Policy
Yale University
310 Prospect Street
New Haven, CT 06511
(203) 432-9931
Sharon Lynn Kagan

Center for Career Development in Early Care and Education
Wheelock College
200 The Riverway
Boston, MA 02215
(617) 734-5200, ext. 211
Andrea Genser, Azra Farrell, Gwen Morgan

Center for Law and Social Policy (CLASP)
1616 P Street, N.W., Suite 450
Washington, D.C. 20036
(202) 328-5140
Mark Greenberg, Steve Savner

Child Care Action Campaign (CCAC)
330 Seventh Avenue, Floor 17
New York, NY 10032
(212) 239-0138
Gail Richardson

Child Care Law Center (CCLC)
22 Second Street, 5th Floor
San Francisco, CA 94105
(415) 495-5498
Kathleen O'Brien

Children's Defense Fund (CDF)
25 E Street, N.W.
Washington, D.C. 20001
(202) 628-8787
Gina Adams, Helen Blank

Children's Foundation
725 15th Street, N.W., Suite 505
Washington, D.C. 20005-2109
(202) 347-3300
Sandy Gellert, Kaye Hollestelle

Council of Chief State School Officers (CCSSO)
One Massachusetts Avenue, N.W., Suite 700
Washington, D.C. 20001-1431
(202) 336-7033
Bill Shephardson

Families and Work Institute
330 Seventh Avenue, 14th floor
New York, NY 10001
(212) 465-2044
Ellen Galinsky, Robin Hardman

High/Scope Educational Research Foundation
600 North River Street
Ypsilanti, MI 48198
(734) 485-2000
Larry Schweinhart

I Am Your Child Campaign
1010 Wisconsin Avenue, N.W., Suite 800
Washington, D.C. 20007
(202) 338-4385
David Smith, Jodi Slusky

National Association for Child Care Resource and Referral Agencies (NACCRRA)
1391 F Street, N.W., Suite 810
Washington, D.C. 20004-1106
(202) 393-5501
Yasmina Vinci

National Center for Children in Poverty
Columbia University School of Public Health
154 Haven Avenue
New York, NY 10032
(212) 927-8793
Jane Knitzer

National Association for the Education of Young Children (NAEYC)
1509 16th Street, N.W.
Washington, D.C. 20036-1426
(202)232-8777
Barbara Willer

National Center for the Early Childhood Workforce (NCECW)
733 15th Street, N.W., Suite 800
Washington, D.C. 20005
(202) 737-0370
Alice Burton

National Child Care Information Center (NCCIC)
301 Maple Avenue West, Suite 602
Vienna, VA 22180
(800) 616-2242
Danielle Ewen

National Conference of State Legislatures (NCSL)
1560 Broadway, Suite 700
Denver, CO 80202
(303) 830-2200
Scott Groginsky, Laurie McConnell

National Dropout Prevention Center
Clemson University
205 Martin Street
Clemson, SC 29634-5111
(864) 656-2599
Dr. Jay Smink

National Economic Development and Law Center
2201 Broadway, Suite 815
Oakland, CA 94612-3024
(510) 251-2600
Janette E. Stokley

National Education Goals Panel
1255 22nd Street, N.W., Suite 502
Washington, D.C. 20037
(202) 632-0952
Emily Wurtz

National Governors' Association (NGA)
444 North Capitol Street, N.W., Suite 250
Washington, D.C. 20001
(202) 624-5300
Helene Stebbins

National Head Start Association
1651 Prince Street
Alexandria, VA 22314
(202) 822-8405
Sarah Greene

National Institute on Out-of-School Time
Center for Research on Women
Wellesley College
106 Central Street
Wellesley, MA 02181-8259
(617) 283-2547
Michelle Seligson, Beth Miller

Zero to Three
2000 14th Sreet, North, Suite 380
Arlington, VA
(703) 528-4300
Bev Jackson, Abbey Griffin

REFERENCES

Adams, Diane, Ruth Anne Foote and Yasmina S. Vinci. *Making Child Care Work: A Study of Child Care Resource and Referral in the United States.* Washington, D.C.: National Association of Child Care Resource and Referral Agencies, 1996.

Adams, Gina, and Nicole Oxendine Poersch, *Who Cares? State Commitment to Child Care and Early Education* (Washington, D.C.: Children's Defense Fund, December 1996).

Adams, Gina, and Jodi Sandfort. *First Steps, Promising Futures: State Prekindergarten Initiatives in the Early 1990s.* Washington, D.C.: Children's Defense Fund, 1994.

Adams, Gina C., and Nicole Oxendine Poersch. *Key Facts About Child Care and Early Education: A Briefing Book.* Washington, D.C.: Children's Defense Fund, 1997.

American Public Welfare Association. *The Child Care Challenge: States Leading the Way, Child Care Status Survey.* Washington, D.C.: APWA, August 1997.

Azer, Sheri L., and Elizabeth Newman. *Connecting the Links: The Career Development Networking Directory.* Boston: The Center for Career Development in Early Care and Education at Wheelock College, undated.

Bellm, Dan, et al. *Making Work Pay in the Child Care Industry: Promising Practices for Improving Compensation.* Washington, D.C.: National Center for the Early Childhood Work Force, 1997.

Blank, Helen. *Helping Parents Work and Children Succeed: A Guide to Child Care and the 1996 Welfare Act.* Washington, D.C.: Children's Defense Fund, 1997.

Carnegie Corporation of New York. *Starting Points: Meeting the Needs of Our Youngest Children.* New York: Carnegie Corporation of New York, April 1994.

Casper, Lynne M. *What Does It Cost to Mind Our Preschoolers?* and *Who's Minding Our Preschoolers?* U.S. Bureau of the Census, Current Population Reports, P70-52 and P70-53. Washington, D.C., September 1995 and March 1996.

Center for Law and Social Policy. *A Summary of Key Child Care Provisions of H.R. 3734: The Personal Responsibility and Work Opportunity Reconciliation Act of 1997.* Washington, D.C.: CLASP, August 1996.

Center for the Future of Children, The David and Lucile Packard Foundation. *The Future of Children Series: Welfare to Work; Financing Child Care; Long-term Outcomes of Early*

Childhood Programs. Volumes 5, 6, 7, nos. 3, 2, 1. Los Altos, Calif.: The David and Lucile Packard Foundation, Winter 1995,Summer/Fall 1996, Spring 1997.

Child Care Bulletin (National Child Care Information Center, Child Care Bureau, Administration on Children, Youth and Families, Department of Health and Human Services), July/August 1997.

"Child Care 1997: How Your State Rates." *Working Mother* magazine, July/August 1997.

Children's Defense Fund. *The State of America's Children Yearbook 1997.* Washington, D.C.: CDF, 1997.

The Children's Foundation. *1996 Family Child Care Licensing Study.* Washington, D.C.: The Children's Foundation, 1996.

The Children's Foundation. *1997 Child Care Center Licensing Study.* Washington, D.C.: The Children's Foundation, 1997.

Cohen, Nancy E., and Sharon L. Kagan. *Funding and Financing Early Care and Education: A Review of Issues and Strategies.* New Haven, Conn.: Yale Bush Center in Child Development and Social Policy, 1997.

Collins, Ann, Stephanie Jones and Heather Bloom. *Children and Welfare Reform: Highlights from Recent Research.* New York: National Center for Children in Poverty, 1996.

Collins, James. "The Day-Care Dilemma." Special Report, *TIME* magazine, February 3, 1997.

Coopers and Lybrand L.L.P. *State of North Carolina Smart Start Program Performance Audit.* North Carolina: Coopers and Lybrand, April 1996.

Cost, Quality and Child Outcomes Study Team. *Cost, Quality, and Child Outcomes in Child Care Centers, Public Report,* second edition. Denver: Economics Department, University of Colorado at Denver, 1995.

Dombro, Amy Laura, et al. *Community Mobilization: Strategies to Support Young Children and Their Families.* New York: Families and Work Institute, 1996.

Galinsky, Ellen, et al. *The Study of Children in Family Child Care and Relative Care: Highlights of Findings.* New York: Families and Work Institute, 1994.

Galinsky, Ellen, James T. Bond and Dana Friedman. *The Changing Workforce: Highlights of the National Study.* New York: Families and Work Institute, 1993.

Gormley Jr., William T. *Everybody's Children: Child Care as a Public Problem.* Washington, D.C.: The Brookings Institution, 1995.

Healthy Child Care America (American Academy of Pediatrics) 1, no. 2 (September 1997).

Howes, Carolee, Ellen Smith and Ellen Galinsky. *The Florida Child Care Quality Improvement Study: Interim Report.* New York: Families and Work Institute, 1995.

Kagan, Sharon L., and Nancy E. Cohen. *Not By Chance: Creating an Early Care and Education System for America's Children.* New Haven, Conn.: The Quality 2000 Initiative, 1997.

Kamerman, Sheila B., and Alfred J. Kahn, eds. *Child Care in the Context of Welfare "Reform."* Report IV. New York: Cross-National Studies Research Program, Columbia University School of Social Work, 1997.

Knitzer, Jane, and Stephen Page. *Map and Track: State Initiatives for Young Children and Families.* New York: National Center for Children in Poverty, Columbia University School of Public Health, 1996.

Larner, Mary. *In the Neighborhood: Programs That Strengthen Family Day Care For Low-Income Families.* New York: National Center for Children in Poverty, Columbia University, 1994.

Legislative Office of Education Oversight. *Implementation of Head Start in Ohio.* Columbus, Ohio: LOEO, April 1997.

Lewis, Sean. *Subsidized Child Care and the Working Poor,* Interim Project Report. Tallahassee, Fl.: Florida House of Representatives, February 1996.

Long, Sharon K., and Sandra J. Clark. "The New Child Care Block Grant: State Funding Choices and Their Implications." *New Federalism: Issues and Options for States* (The Urban Institute), series A, no. A-12 (October 1997).

Miller, Beth M. *Out-of-School Time: Effects on Learning in the Primary Grades,* SACC Action Research Paper #4. Wellesley Mass.: School-Age Child Care Project, Center for Research on Women, June 1995.

Mitchell, Anne, Louise Stoney and Harriet Dichter. *Financing Child Care in the United States: An Illustrative Catalog of Current Strategies.* Philadelphia: The Ewing Marion Kauffman Foundation and The Pew Charitable Trusts, 1997.

Morgan, Gwen, et al. *Making a Career of It: The State of the States Report on Career Development In Early Care and Education.* Boston: The Center for Career Development in Early Care and Education at Wheelock College, 1993.

Nash, J. Madeline. "Fertile Minds." Special Report, *TIME* magazine, February 3, 1997.

National Association of Child Care Resource and Referral Agencies. *Supporting Families In Changing Times: CCR&R Looks to the Future.* Washington, D.C.: NACCRRA, 1996.

National Governor's Association. *The First Three Years: A Governor's Guide to Early Childhood.* Washington, D.C.: National Governor's Association, 1997.

Nussbaum, Karen. *Care Around the Clock: Developing Child Care Resources Before Nine and After Five.* Washington, D.C.: U.S. Department of Labor, 1995.

Phillips, Deborah, and Anne Bridgman, eds. *New Findings on Children, Families, and Economic Self-Sufficiency: Summary of a Research Briefing.* Washington, D.C.: National Academy Press, 1995.

Poersch, Nicole Oxedine, and Helen Blank. *Working Together for Children: Head Start and Child Care Partnerships.* Washington, D.C.: Children's Defense Fund, January 1996.

"Recruiting Welfare Recipients for Child Care Work: Not a Panacea." *Working for Change* (The Child Care Law Center, San Francisco), 1996.

Rohacek, Monica H., and Susan D. Russell. *Child Care Subsidy: An Investment Strategy for North Carolina.* Carrboro, N.C.: December 1996.

Rosmarin, Ada Pollock, et al. *School-Age Care: Out of School Time,* Resource Notebook developed for the Child Care Technical Assistance Project. Washington, D.C.: Child Care Bureau, Administration for Children and Families, March 1997.

Schweinhart, Lawrence J., Helen V. Barnes and David P. Weikart. *Significant Benefits: The High/Scope Perry Preschool Study Through Age 27.* Ypsilanti, Mich.: High/Scope Press, 1993.

Shore, Rima. *Rethinking the Brain: New Insights into Early Development.* New York: Families and Work Institute,1997.

Smith, Shelley L., Mary Fairchild, and Scott Groginsky. *Early Childhood Care and Education: An Investment that Works,* second edition. Denver: National Conference of State Legislatures, 1997.

State of Colorado. *Report of the Colorado Business Commission on Child Care Financing.* Denver: State of Colorado, December 1995.

Stoney, Louise. *Giving Children a Strong Start: Effective Early Childhood Policy in the States.* Denver, Colo.: Education Commission of the States, 1997.

Stoney, Louise. *Promoting Access To Quality Child Care: Critical Steps in Conducting Market Rate Surveys and Establishing Rate Policies.* Washington, D.C.: Children's Defense Fund, August 1994.

United States General Accounting Office. *Child Care Subsidies Increase Likelihood That Low-Income Mothers Will Work.* Washington, D.C.: U.S. GAO, December 1994.

Whitebook, Marcy, Laura Sakai, and Carollee Howes. *NAEYC Accreditation as a Strategy for Improving Child Care Quality.* Washington, D.C.: National Center for the Early Childhood Workforce, 1997.

"Your Child From Birth to Three." Special Edition, *Newsweek,* Spring/Summer 1997.

About the Authors

Mary L. Culkin is an assistant research professor at the University of Colorado Health Sciences Center, School of Nursing, and an adjunct professor at the Naropa Institute. Her involvement in the development of several programs for young children and their families led to a research focus on cost and quality relationships in early childhood services. She is involved in research about leadership and administration in early childhood programs.

Scott Groginsky is a senior policy specialist with the National Conference of State Legislatures' Children and Families Program. He coordinates the Early Childhood Care and Education Project that provides information services, legislative training sessions and a variety of technical assistance to legislators who are interested in improving early childhood systems. He has written the issue briefs, *Child Care for Low-Income Families* and *Child Care and the Transition Off Welfare,* and co-authored the article, "An Ounce of Prevention" in NCSL's *State Legislatures* magazine. He co-authored the first and second editions of *Early Childhood Care and Education: An Investment That Works.* He holds a bachelor of arts degree in political science from The George Washington University.

Steve Christian is a policy specialist with the National Conference of State Legislatures' Children and Families Program and coordinates the Child Welfare Project. He is the author of *New Directions for Child Protective Services: Supporting Children, Families and Communities Through Legislative Reform.* He holds a law degree from the University of Virginia and a masters degree in social work from the University of Denver.

INDEX